BEYOND LEARNING BY DOING

riential
ıg, and
ding of

niversity

)es this
t going
oretical

ncom–
ıcation
lds has
ressive
doing"
sumed
ectives
ıw the
social

e field,
oretical
urrent

Jay W. Roberts is an Associate Professor of Education and Environmental Studies at Earlham College in Richmond, Indiana.

BEYOND LEARNING BY DOING

Theoretical Currents in Experiential Education

Jay W. Roberts

Routledge
Taylor & Francis Group

NEW YORK AND LONDON

First published 2012
by Routledge
711 Third Avenue, New York, NY 10017

Simultaneously published in the UK
by Routledge
2 Park Square, Milton Park, Abingdon, Oxon OX14 4RN

Routledge is an imprint of the Taylor & Francis Group, an informa business

Library of Congress Cataloging-in-Publication Data
Roberts, Jay W.
    Beyond learning by doing : theoretical currents in experiential education /
Jay W. Roberts.
        p. cm.
    Includes bibliographical references and index.
    1. Experiential learning. 2. Active learning. I. Title.
    LB1027.23.R63 2011
    370.15′23—dc22   2011012423

ISBN13: 978-0-415-88207-1 (hbk)
ISBN13: 978-0-415-88208-8 (pbk)
ISBN13: 978-0-203-84808-1 (ebk)

Typeset in Bembo by
Keystroke, Station Road, Codsall, Wolverhampton
Printed and bound in the United States of America on acid-free paper by
Walsworth Publishing Company, Marceline, MO.

SUSTAINABLE
FORESTRY
INITIATIVE

Certified Sourcing
www.sfiprogram.org
SFI-00555
The SFI label applies to the text stock.

To my "girls" (EJR, AMR, and MDR).
You are my hopeful current.

CONTENTS

PREFACE

Time is but the stream I go a-fishing in. Its thin current slides away, but
eternity remains.

Henry David Thoreau

Home Water

Every fisherman has a home water. Mine is the east fork of the Whitewater River
as it winds due south through the grey Ordovician limestone and verdant
agricultural fields of east-central Indiana to eventually join up with the mighty
Ohio just outside Cincinnati. On the days when I am lucky enough to steal away
for several hours, I throw my gear into the back of "Rose," my trusted 1993
Toyota Tercel, the same car I have had since graduating from college, and head
down US Highway 27 through small, iconic Midwestern towns like Liberty,
Indiana, where the county courthouse still looms large over the town center. I
always perk up as I crest the final hill and head down into the town of Brookville,
where the Whitewater re-emerges below the Brookville Dam, a Corps of
Engineers project in the 1960s, and heads down through the small town and into
one of the prettiest stretches of water in the state. It's a rare thing to get a "view"
in east-central Indiana, but this stretch of road offers a good one. Often, early
morning fog still rests on the river, and the surrounding hills and countryside lift
up out of that grey blanket to offer a sense of being above the clouds in some
higher, ethereal plain.

In that small moment in time, the world is awash in possibilities. There are
innumerable fish to be hooked and brought to the net, or, just as well, hooked
and lost. Even if it ends up being a slow day on the water, perhaps I will catch a
glimpse of a bald eagle perched in the sycamore tree near the river bend. Or,

maybe the family of otters will make their presence known on the sandbar. I am lucky to have a home water. When I travel, sometimes I have the chance to fish other, more famous waters. There is unquestionably a joy and a certain sense of adventure that comes with fishing a classic river, one that has been written about in countless magazines and guidebooks. Yet the wondrous thing about a home water is that it is the one you always return to. It is the one you know the best. Home waters hold an intimacy and a physical connection well beyond the exotic nature of more distant, famous rivers. It is for this reason that, despite the allure of rivers with grander settings and bigger fish, I feel most at peace fishing the two-mile section of the east-fork of the Whitewater River. It is my home water.

In a very similar sense, experiential education is also my "home water." I entered into teaching through the field of experiential education and, despite my wanderings far and wide, inevitably find myself returning to it, feeling more at home and at peace within its confines then in any other theoretical or practical discipline. While in college, I stumbled into a summer camp job in a northern suburb of Chicago between my junior and senior years. I had been studying abroad during the previous spring and had not managed to line up a more serious job so I settled for working a summer overnight camp near where my parents lived. As it turned out, my job that summer likely directed the course of my life ever since. Working as a camp counselor in this academic enrichment camp, I witnessed remarkable changes and shifts in children who were labeled as "at-risk." Middle-school and high-school students who came into the camp extremely angry or disengaged with formal schooling would leave with a stronger sense of self, a growing self-confidence, and a renewed love of learning. It was unlike anything I had experienced previously in my own schooling. The educational environment was highly interactive and loaded with meaning as camp leaders and counselors wove personal skills seamlessly with more "academic" work. One particular highlight was the "challenge education" day where students would experience a full day's worth of high and low ropes course events which were carefully framed and tied into changing their limiting mental models of themselves and their view of school. I came away from that summer tremendously moved and impressed with the potential power of this sort of educational approach. What was this style of education called? Where did it come from? Who else is doing similar things? Questions spun around in my head as I attempted to place what I had experienced in the larger context of education and schooling. I ended up working for the company that operated that camp for nine years, traveling all over the country, even helping run a camp in Hong Kong in the late 1990s.

Yet, even as I was immersed in the practice of this transformational style of learning, I remained curious about the underlying theory and philosophy of the approach. I began to look around for conferences and other professional development opportunities that dealt with this particular (and peculiar) notion of education. It was through that process that I came to learn about the "field" of experiential education. Thrilled that I finally had a specific name and territory to work from, I began branching out, working for other organizations and companies that associated themselves with experiential education. I worked as an outdoor educator teaching skiing, climbing, and other technical skills to youth and adults in Illinois and Minnesota. I directed a high and low ropes course program at a large state university in Virginia. I moonlighted as a consultant, facilitating corporate work teams through team building and leadership initiatives and worked with at-risk alcohol and drug-abuse populations in experiential contexts. Through it all I remained as passionate as ever about the power and even "magic" of the experiential approach I learned about during that summer camp job in college. Yet, as I continued on in my newfound career, I also began to have concerns. Not all of the educational moments I experienced with students were as transformative as I assumed they would be. I began to grow somewhat weary and skeptical of "yet another four hour ropes course program." Sure, the participants enjoyed themselves and said all the right things in the debriefs about the importance of trust, communication, and the like but I had my doubts about how much of this was sincere or would persist beyond the initial experience.

From these first, tentative misgivings, I began to more thoroughly examine and interrogate the theory behind the practice. I went back to school and, as part of my graduate course of study, began to explore the broader field of educational philosophy. When I attended professional conferences in experiential and outdoor education, I found myself gravitating away from the sessions on practice and experiential methods and toward the ones on experiential theory. What I found disturbed me. After learning about the depth and rigor of the educational philos-ophy of John Dewey and other progressive-minded scholars in graduate school, I was disappointed at what appeared to be a lack of theoretical grounding in the field. Attempts to explain the philosophical roots and foundations of the field seemed shallow at best and mischaracterizations at worst. The field of experiential education appeared long on practice and very short on theory. As I continued on in my career, my concerns about the lack of theoretical grounding and the subsequent vulnerability of the practice grew stronger and more persistent. My skepticism of the "transformative" potential of experiential education began to overshadow my earlier positive memories of that first summer camp experience. I found it difficult to even get excited about the work itself anymore. When a tenure-track position in education with an emphasis in experiential learning came up at a small liberal-arts college in Indiana, I accepted it, hoping it would help move me out of my theoretical and practical "funk" in relation to my field. Yet, the move did not resolve the tensions I felt between the theory and practice of experiential education. It only placed them in greater relief as I began to explore how this notion of experience in education intersects with a variety of curricular projects from outdoor and adventure education, to environmental education and service learning. It was clear to me that, while there was a wide range of literature on the *practice* of experiential education, scholarly and philosophical work on the *theory* was significantly lacking.

However, despite these misgivings, experiential education remains very much my "home water." While I grow frustrated, at times, with the state of affairs in the field, I continue to return to it, finding new ways to engage and find my place. One such place of engagement for me is this book. As I looked around at the state of the field of experiential education, one of the things that seemed most glaringly absent was a theoretical work from a single, narrative voice. There are a small number of "theory" and "philosophy" books on experiential education, but almost all of them are compilations of individual articles or chapters. While there is worth to such efforts, particularly as they provide a greater diversity of theoretical perspectives and arguments than any single-authored work could, I think the reader misses out on the opportunity to delve deeply into experience through the eyes of one author, as he or she sees it. This book is my humble attempt to do just that.

ACKNOWLEDGEMENTS

It is difficult at this point in journey, looking back on the six years of work that led to this book, to properly put into words the many people and encounters I have had that made their mark on this project. There are simply too many to thank and acknowledge. But a few words are necessary. To my partner and wife, none of this would have been possible without your steadfast support and hard work helping keep everything running. My colleagues and the students at Earlham serve as my inspiration and my learning laboratory. So many of the thoughts that make up these pages come from discussions, debates, and interactions I have had with the wonderful people that make up that special place. More thanks go to those that supported me during my graduate work and my dissertation at Miami University—Richard Quantz and Kathleen Knight-Abowitz in particular. Finally, to my parents, who have throughout my life shown me what good teaching is all about, this book is as much about what you have inspired in me as anything.

A special note of thanks also goes to my principal editor at Routledge, Naomi Silverman, who believed in this project and provided support and encouragement along the way.

1

INTRODUCTION

The River of Experience

I am large, I contain multitudes.

Walt Whitman, "Song of Myself"

Stepping in to the River

From afar, rivers can take on a homogeneous appearance. I remember standing on the south rim of the Grand Canyon once, looking down on the Colorado River thousands of feet below. From that viewpoint, it looked like an impossibly blue ribbon that had been carefully placed on the rust-orange of the canyon floor. No variations were apparent, nothing to suggest movement, impediments, or dynamism. Yet, after two hard days of hiking, I saw a very different river as I stood next to the raging torrent of its shores. Here, the Colorado was no decorative ribbon, it was alive, pulsing, charging, and shifting in seemingly endless directions with color patterns of foam, soil, and sky. Understanding such as this required intimacy and exploration. It could not have come from the rim, no matter how carefully I observed or how long I spent. Standing on the rim of the Grand Canyon, one can easily take much for granted. How hard it will be to hike down (and, more importantly back up). How hot it is down on the canyon floor. How dynamic the landscape becomes during a sudden rainstorm. To really *see* the Grand Canyon and the main shaping force of the Colorado River, the rim is not sufficient. And yet, the vast majority of tourists and visitors to the national park never leave the rim. They arrive in cars, pull over at various lookout points, take in the scenery, snap a few photos, and drive off having never ventured down into the details.

To organize a project such as this, metaphors can be of real use—they can guide both the author and the reader, providing meaningful anchors along the theoretical journey while (hopefully) maintaining a narrative coherence. Maxine Greene and Morwenna Griffiths (2003) in their essay "Feminism, Philosophy, and Education: Imagining Public Spaces" discuss the power of metaphorical thinking (p. 85):

> We need to rethink, to think differently: to use our imaginations again . . . metaphorical language [is] a way of rethinking and questioning orthodox thinking. A metaphor is what it does. A metaphor, because of the way it brings together things that are unlike, reorients consciousness.

This book is about stepping off the rim and hiking down into the details. And, it is about realizing that the heretofore homogeneous looking "river" of experience employed in experiential education is actually much more complex and varied than perhaps previously thought. For too long, the concept of experiential education has stayed, metaphorically, "on the rim." Theoretical and philosophical inquiries have been few and often too shallow to fully explore the diversity and range of currents in our river of experience. As a result, much of the conversation and curriculum theorizing in experiential education takes the central organizing concept—that of experience—for granted. This shallow theorizing is not just a mere oversight, it has real consequences to the ways we envision the future possibilities of the educational and schooling endeavor. A river without variations, without movement, becomes stagnant—a fetid backwater incapable of supporting a vibrant and diverse community of life. So, rather than an assumed single and relatively static theoretical current, I will contend that this "river" of experience is made up of many, sometimes contradictory, currents and perspectives. As Whitman describes, "I am large, I contain multitudes." My hope is that using this metaphor will allow us, as Greene and Griffiths suggest, to "think differently" as it relates to experiential education. The taken-for-granted sense that we all know what we mean when we evoke the power of experience in the educational process needs to be unveiled. It is time to use our imaginations again when it comes to considering the role of experience in education.

In order to begin this work, we must first articulate a bit of background and context around this enigmatic term "experiential education" as it has been the focus of much debate, confusion, and misconception. First, we'll need to make some distinctions in nomenclature between the terms "learning by doing" and "experiential education." Second, we'll place experiential education in context as a particular field of activity in curriculum theorizing. And third, we'll consider where and when this particular strand of progressivism emerged. Articulating the contexts of experiential education will hopefully ensure that we can begin on more or less solid ground, before venturing into the shifting sands and turbulent waters of the theoretical currents themselves.

Beyond Learning by Doing

If the theoretical development of experiential education can be summed up in some form of an overarching exploration, it is the on-going quest to define itself.

Ironically, for a field steeped in Deweyian pragmatism, thinkers and practitioners have long labored over a sort of "quest for certainty" in terms of bounding and operationalizing the term "experiential education." Indeed, there is little consensus on what, in fact, experiential education is. It has been alternatively described as "adventure education," "outdoor education," "challenge education," and "environmental education" (Adkins & Simmons, 2002; Priest & Miles, 1990). The American Educational Research Association (AERA) includes such Special Interest Groups (SIGs) as "Ecological and Environmental Education," "Outdoor and Adventure Education," and "Service Learning and Experiential Education." Richard Louv (2005) labels it a "movement" in *Last Child in the Woods*: "[t]he definitions and nomenclature of this movement are tricky. In recent decades, the approach has gone by many names: community-oriented schooling, bioregional education, experiential education, and, most recently, place-based or environment-based education" (p. 204). How could curricular approaches as varied as "adventure education" and "community-oriented schooling" be considered the same thing?

To further muddy up the water, practical applications of experiential education are numerous and varied. Certainly we might consider each of the following as examples of experiential education: taking a field trip, working cooperatively in a group on a project, volunteering in the community, completing a lab experiment, or learning to ride a bike. Each of these learning activities involves some degree of experience as part of the process. But then, doesn't *all* learning involve experience? If so, have we created a sort of tautology here? That is, can we only define experiential education as "education that involves experience"? If so, we haven't really articulated anything at all. Surely, not *all* education is experiential education. As evidenced by Louv and the examples listed above, people do seem to have a common-sense framework that they draw from in articulating what experiential education is. Experiential education is more of a "something" than an "everything." What that "something" is will be the subject of this book. Yet in order to begin to flesh it out we have to clear up some misconceptions. The first is the distinction between experiential "learning" and experiential "education."

Most often, experiential education is framed as "learning by doing." So, in the practical examples articulated above (lab experiments, riding a bike, field trips), each of these relates to the other in the sense that they all involve some form of experiential *learning*. This can be equated to our metaphor of the "view from the rim." From here, things look fairly simple and straightforward. But even the most cursory glance at all the possible variations of education and learning that would count as "experiential" under this definition would reveal its inadequacies. As Itin (1999, p. 91) claims:

> Meaningful discussions have been . . . hampered in that the terms [experiential education and experiential learning] have been used to describe many different teaching approaches, work experiences, outdoor education, adventure education, vocational education, lab work . . . [and that] experiential education and experiential learning have often been used synonymously with these other terms.

So here we have a key distinction that must be understood before we proceed. Experiential education is not experiential learning. While there may be a variety of educational contexts that employ experiential *learning* (what I call learning by doing), this does not necessarily mean experiential *education* is a part of the process. What is the difference? We might think of learning as knowledge or skill acquired by instruction or study. This can happen either in formal schooling contexts or in informal settings outside of school (such as learning to ride a bike). Education, from the Latin root *educare*, to lead out, on the other hand, implies a broader *process* of what Richard Rorty called "individuation and socialization" (1999). Education, properly conceived, involves important questions about the structure and function of knowledge, the ethical imperatives of such knowledge, and the purposes to which learning ought to adhere. Thus education, as a process of both individuation and socialization, is rooted in longstanding philosophical queries as to the nature of self and society. Experiential learning, on the other hand, can be seen as a *method* or *technique* that any teacher might employ to meet certain instructional objectives. For example, an English teacher might help students learn rhyme and meter by asking them to "dance out" a poem in iambic pentameter. This is certainly "learning by doing" or the use of experiential learning in the moment. But it does not necessarily follow that using this method is the same as the *process* of experiential education as articulated by John Dewey (1938) and others. The two ask fundamentally different questions and work in different domains.

It should be noted that learning by doing as a method or technique is not without merit. Research supports the educational effectiveness of novelty, emotion, and challenge often associated with experiential environments (Bransford, 2000; Caine & Caine, 1991). Teaching techniques that support cooperative interaction and active student engagement have been championed in the popular literature on educational reform (Sizer, 1997; Meier, 1995; Fried, 2001). Certainly, many effective teachers understand the importance of mixing it up in the classroom and providing opportunities for students to learn in a wide variety of styles and methods—one of which may be experiential. Educators have long relied on the experiential approaches mentioned above (and many others) to create enriched learning environments for students.

Yet, while there is nothing categorically wrong with this particular construction of experience in education, it does come with limitations. In this frame of reference, experiential methods or activities are used as a technique available to the teacher (among a wide variety of other techniques such as direct instruction,

Socratic seminar, small group work, etc.). For example, "hands-on" activities are used to break up the monotony of direct instruction or to bring to life specific content areas. Field trips are used to "get kids out of the classroom." Or, experiential activity can be seen as accessing a type of kinesthetic intelligence (Gardner, 1993) or learning modality that teachers ought to use to reach a variety of different learning styles. What all these methods have in common is the manner in which experience is technically defined and applied. That is to say, the experience is tightly bounded (in both time and space) and efficiently controlled. Experience becomes not organic, interactive, and continuous but rather a scripted, timed, and located "activity." Normal classroom or school processes stop and "experiential" activity then begins for a bounded and specific timeframe. Equating experiential education with "learning by doing" in this way frames the way we think and as a result it has particular consequences for the way we enact educational projects. As Paul Hawken (2007) argues, "what we already know frames what we see, and what we see frames what we understand" (p. 15). In many ways, experiential education, when framed as "learning by doing," becomes equated with a method or a technique. It becomes a useful tool in the hands of the teacher—something to be employed in small chunks, but not functionally altering the broader purposes and aims of education and school. It does not get at the philosophical queries about the purposes of schooling and structure and function of knowledge described earlier. It is also vulnerable to caricature and over-simplification. Just like the tourists on the rim who look out, snap a quick picture, and perhaps even declare "I thought it would be bigger" as they drive away, limiting our viewpoint of experiential education to "learning by doing" lends itself to shallow thinking. E. D. Hirsch, for example, in his seminal and influential text *The Schools We Need and Why We Don't Have Them*, defines learning by doing as "a phrase once used to characterize the progressivist movement but little used today, possibly because the formulation has been the object of much criticism and even ridicule" (1996, p. 256). Surely, there must be more to experiential education than mere activity and method? There is. And it is this broader and potentially deeper articulation of experiential education that we turn to next.

The Field of Experiential Education

So, we have taken care of one misconception—that of equating experiential education with experiential learning. But this leaves us with another. If experiential education is not simply a method to be used by a teacher in an instructional moment, what is it? Itin (1999) argues that, properly understood, experiential education is a *philosophy*. He states (p. 97):

> if experiential education is correctly identified as a philosophy, it allows for
> the various expressions of this philosophy (service learning, cooperative

learning, adventure-based, problem-based, action learning, etc.) to be linked together under this single philosophy. This provides a method for bringing those together who promote these various expressions and to argue for educational reform that would support experiential education in all settings.

Framing experiential education as a philosophy, to Itin, avoids the vulnerabilities of equating it with a method or technique while at the same time allowing for a number of curricular projects to find a coherent home underneath its conceptual framework. This seems like a good, useful move. However, there are problems here as well. A "philosophy" of education has to sit on its own in terms of its epistemological, ethical, and ontological assumptions. Experiential education, as we will see here, draws from a variety of *other* philosophies and, as such, ought to be seen as derivative of them and not a philosophy in and of itself. So if we can't exactly call it a philosophy, what is it?

As I mentioned in the introduction to this chapter, the defining characteristic of the theoretical explorations of experiential education has been on-going quest for definition. But, in many ways, experiential education is a sort of *tabula rasa*, a blank slate from which we project our hopes, fears, and assumptions about education and schooling. How we choose to frame it, define it, and conceptualize it says as much about us as it does about some objective reality out there. As Capra (1997) noted in a different context, "We never speak about [it] without at the same time speaking about ourselves" (p. 77). I don't make any claims that this theoretical exploration will somehow capture or retrieve some truer or more accurate sense of what experiential education "is." As Martin Jay (2005) states regarding uncovering a "correct" notion of experience in his excellent work, *Songs of Experience* (p. 3):

> Rather than force a totalized account, which assumes a unified point of departure, an etymological arche to be recaptured, or a normative telos to be achieved, it will be far more productive to follow disparate threads where they may lead us. Without the burden of seeking to rescue or legislate a single acceptation of the word, we will be free to uncover and explore its multiple and often contradictory meanings and begin to make sense of how and why they function as they often have to produce such a powerful effect.

So, if we avoid attempting to "legislate a single acceptation" of experiential education, where does that leave us in terms of exploring this theoretical landscape?

If experiential education is not a method and it is not a philosophy and yet at the same time we need to avoid legislating a single definition of the term, how can we speak of it? This is the difficulty of employing such a philosophically enigmatic term such as "experience" and combining it with another enigmatic term: "education." For the purposes of this book, it will be most useful to refer to experiential education as a field.

As Rumi writes: "Out beyond ideas of wrongdoing and rightdoing there is a field. I'll meet you there" (Barks, 1995). Defining the boundaries of what might be considered experiential education is a tricky task for all the reasons stated above. If we take Rumi's advice about avoiding "wrongdoing and rightdoing" we are left, in his words, with a field. And this, I contend, is just the way to view experiential education. Not as a method, or a philosophy, or a movement, but as a *field*. Merriam Webster defines a field as "an area or division of an activity, subject, or profession" (http://www.merriam-webster.com/netdict/field, retrieved February 10, 2010). We can think of a variety of "fields" as examples including academic disciplines (e.g. History or Mathematics), professions (e.g. Nursing or Engineering), or subject interests held in common (e.g. bird watching or the culinary arts). In each of these cases, it is reasonable to bound the interests and activities as a "field" to signify common intellectual roots, activities, and/or subject of study. For the purposes of this book, I will choose to call experiential education a "field" because, I believe, there exist common intellectual roots, activities, and a subject of study that holds the disparate, visible curriculum projects together. This is not to suggest that tensions or contradictions within the field do not exist. Fields do not presume homogeneity or consensus, only a common space within which questions are raised, answers are sought, and the overall inquiry is engaged. Unlike philosophies, fields need not be as coherent and, in fact, are often quite eclectic as is the case with the field of experiential education. Yet the eclecticism has its own character—a "something" rather than an "everything." To return to our working metaphor of the river, while the currents within the river may be distinct and identifiable, they exist, collectively, as a single river. They are held together by the banks which exist to define and bound the river as a single entity. Thus, while it is possible to speak of a variety of theoretical currents and curriculum projects here, it is also possible to speak of a single field that bounds and holds these together.

So what comprises the field of experiential education? It is surprisingly diverse. Some projects use nature and the outdoors as the central focus including outdoor education, challenge education, and adventure education. These projects often look to historical figures such as Kurt Hahn, the founder of Outward Bound, and environmental writers such as Thoreau, John Muir, Aldo Leopold, and Rachel Carson, as intellectual antecedents. Other projects focus more on the experiential learning cycle as a process, irrespective of context, drawing from the work of early educational progressives such as John Dewey and William Kilpatrick or, in the contemporary context, the work of David Kolb. There are even hybrids such as place-based education, service learning, and expeditionary learning that seem to draw from both traditions. And, it could be argued that some of these might be seen as separate fields in and of themselves. This certainly appears to be the case with environmental education and service learning, for example. It is simply not possible to draw a neat and clean genealogy of the field of experiential education and it would be unwise to attempt to do so. As Glenn Savage (2010) noted in another context, there is a "fabulous haze" that surrounds the term. Nonetheless, these various projects *do* have something in common. All of them, in some form or another, lift up the power of experience in the educational process (not just employing it as a technique or method). It is this belief in the educative power of experience, of direct contact, that becomes the warp thread linking the disparate strands together. And, curiously, it is the single *least* interrogated concept in the field.

Conclusion

So, how might we go beyond learning by doing? Are there other ways of thinking about experiential education that might, as Greene and Griffiths suggest, allow us to "use our imaginations again" and "reorient consciousness"? If experiential education is more than "learning by doing," what is it? Stepping off the rim and hiking down to the river, we see something very different. On the banks we see that the river, while still a single entity, is actually composed of many different currents. There are stronger currents and weaker ones, currents that spin and currents that surge up making waves and whitewater. There are even counter-currents, eddies that run up against the main thrust of the flow. In the same sense, once we leave behind "learning by doing" as the central descriptor of experiential education, we see that there is much more variety and heterogeneity than previously thought. Our "river of experience" is actually made up of several distinctive currents. Certainly there is overlap. The currents do not exist independently of one another. In fact, they interact. The currents and counter-currents come into contact with one another, forming eddies and confluences. But they are also nonetheless distinct. It is also possible to "read" these currents. Were it not so, rafters, canoeists, and whitewater kayakers would have a tough time navigating safe passage down the rivers they enjoy. The aim of this book is to read these currents, noting how they are distinct and the points at which they interact with one another.

Why is this work important? Josef Stalin once famously remarked, "ideas are more dangerous than guns, we took away their guns, why should we let them have their ideas?" As a philosopher, I believe that ideas matter. As someone who has practiced experiential education is a variety of contexts for almost twenty years, I have also witnessed first hand the practical implications of various theoretical orientations. As I will argue in this book, limiting experiential education to "learning by doing" leaves the field vulnerable to cooptation and trivialization. When we lose the intellectual diversity that comprises the range of ways we might think and talk about experience in education, we are left speaking a single, increasingly isolated language. History shows us that language isolates are eventually dead languages. They may hold on for a time, increasingly defensive and dogmatic, but eventually they die off, incapable of being maintained as a living language, connected and interactive with the world around it. I see evidence of this in the field of experiential education. It is, despite the best of intentions, a very white, privileged community. In an increasingly polyglot world, a world of plurality, speaking an isolated language only serves to marginalize. Yet, at the same time, we must also defend against the processes of homogeneity at a larger scale. Few believe, for example, that the world would be better off if we all spoke English. How do we protect local diversity in a globalized world? How do we hang on to the distinctive ways experiential education frames the educational process while at the same time ensuring that it does not become quaint and overly isolated? While there are no easy answers to these questions, we must not forget "the ideas that move the stone." This is the role of philosophy. Ideas matter. For experiential education to remain vibrant and relevant, we must not forget the ideas that make visible the variety of curriculum projects we see today. And, the more we explore the remarkable diversity of those ideas, the more opportunities exist to form solidarity with others, to patch together a quilt that "imagines things otherwise" again.

Thus, what follows is a conceptual project that aims to examine the notion of experience as it is employed in the field of experiential education. I begin it as a way of adding understanding to a field that desperately needs more work in this area. But, I also enter into this project personally as well. While I may never be able to reclaim the innocence of my youthful camp memories in terms of believing in the transformative power of experiential education, I do wish to come to terms with what, if anything, I can believe in again. I often fear that my skepticism may slide into cynicism, about the "power" of experience in education, about equal opportunity in schooling, and about the democratic potential in education. It is my personal aim to come to a place of hope again about what we might be able to do, as progressives, in a world of deep injustice and inequality. I am not at all sure that I will get there through this process. But, in the truly pragmatic sense, I aim to try. I do not hope to come to some final and terminal answer as to what experience is as it relates to experiential education. Rather, I hope to open experience in education up to a much broader exploration and construction. This, in the end, presents opportunities. Deconstruction and critique does not have to be destructive. It can be reconstructive, in the classic Deweyan sense. Once we have laid bare the limitations of our current thinking, we have the opportunity to imagine new ways to go forward, with eyes wide open.

In Chapter 2, "Headwaters," I explore the philosophical foundations of experience. This might give the reader some pause, as any attempt in a chapter (never mind an entire book) to "cover" the philosophical history of a concept such as experience would seem foolhardy at best. As I will discuss, the very term "experience" is a veritable tar pit of despair to many a philosopher who has tried to offer the definitive work on the subject. Rest assured, I will make no claims of comprehensiveness here. Rather, in this chapter I aim to engage with those figures that, in my mind, deal most directly with matters of experience and education in ways that specifically illuminate the project at hand. After laying that groundwork, Chapters 3 through 5 will explore three distinct "currents" of experience employed within the field of experiential education. Importantly, they do not hold equal weight, or, to extend the metaphor again, the currents have varying levels of strength in our river. In fact, at least one of them may be seen as a "counter-current," a body of moving water that runs against the main thrust. Each chapter will explore the theoretical scaffolding that holds up each particular construction of experience used in varying degrees in experiential education: Romanticism, pragmatism, and critical theory. Again, these three currents are certainly not the only ones in this river of experience we will be exploring. A project such as this necessitates choices, and the reader will have to decide what is conspicuous in its absence here. Certainly, there is much to be learned from at least one theoretical history that I will not cover in much detail in this book: post-structuralism. This current draws most directly from deconstructions and critiques of experience and the role of language in mediating "authentic" experience. I have chosen not to explore it in much depth in this book as the field of experiential education has yet to meaningfully connect to this current. Yet, there is clearly much to be learned from an engagement with this particular intellectual tradition.[1]

The final two chapters make a more normative (or ethical) claim about experience in education and schooling. Chapter 6 examines the ways in which experience has become commodified into what, in German, has been called *Erlebnisgesellschaft*, or experience-driven society (Jay 2005). Such a construction is, I will argue, colonizing other currents and variations of experience in education and schooling. Countering such a shift ought to become, to me, the central theoretical and practical project for those who work for the democratic aims of experience in education and it is this argument that I take up in the concluding chapter. Here, I combine both the social, democratic elements of Dewey's vision from Chapter 3 with the critical elements developed in Chapter 6 to argue for a form of "Critical Pragmatism" as it relates to experience and schooling. This frame of experience in education renews a sense of democratic experiential education as a means of both resisting the negative aspects of modernism and capitalism as well as creating an ethical platform for the advancement of positive freedom through education. Drawing from these orientations, I hope not to prescribe solutions, but rather to articulate a clear and pressing danger to experiential education (and educational progressivism more broadly) and to

---

1 I would point the reader to several seminal works in this area: Claudia Ruitenberg (2005), "Deconstructing the Experience of the Local: Towards a Radical Pedagogy of Place," Joan Scott (1991), "The Evidence of Experience," and Elizabeth Ellsworth (1989), "Why Doesn't This Feel Empowering?".

illuminate the role experience might play in imagining new, creative, and useful ways forward. Like most pragmatists, I am disinclined to offer universal and technical solutions to values-based problems that are deeply contextual and contingent. There is no "five-point plan" for ensuring the democratic flourishing of experiential education. In the words of Maria Rainer Rilke in his poem, "Letters to a Young Poet" (1986, p. 4):

> Be patient toward all that is unresolved in your heart and try to love the *questions* themselves . . . Do not now seek the answers, which cannot be given you because you would not be able to live them. And the point is, to live everything. *Live* the questions now. Perhaps you will then gradually, without noticing it, live along some distant day into the answer.

In the end, it is the questions themselves that ought to guide us. In many ways, each of the currents discussed here signals to larger discourses within educational and social theory. While it may be true that there is no one "right" current of experience within experiential education, there are certainly consequences to each in regards to both theory and practice. Celebrating the variations does not excuse us from our ethical obligations or choices. Each of the currents laid out in this analysis has real consequences for students, teachers, and all citizens. Let the journey begin.

2

HEADWATERS

From Experience to Experiential Education

I remarked incidentally that the philosophy in question is, to paraphrase the saying of Lincoln about democracy, one of education of, by, and for experience. Not one of these words, *of*, *by*, and *for*, names anything which is self-evident. Each of them is a challenge to discover and put into operation a principle or order of organization which follows from understanding what educational experience signifies.

John Dewey

Introduction

It is well beyond the scope of this project to survey the deep and complex history of experience as a concept in philosophical thought. Moreover, even if one were to take a more focused approach to the ways in which the concept of experience has been evoked within educational discourses, this leaves us with a landscape far too deep and wide to attempt a comprehensive account. To add to the challenge, the very concept of "experience" itself is perhaps one of the most contested in philosophy. Indeed, it led Hans-Georg Gadamer (2001) to say that the concept of experience is "one of the most obscure we have" (p. 310). Michael Oakeshott (1933) described the challenge this way: "experience, of all the words in the philosophic vocabulary is the most difficult to manage . . . and it must be the ambition of every writer reckless enough to use the word to escape the ambiguity it contains" (p. 9). Dewey (1981) himself, in a revised edition of *Experience and Nature*, almost gave up on the concept out of frustration with the way his notion of experience was misinterpreted at the time: "I would abandon the term 'experience' because of my growing realization that the historical obstacles which prevented understanding . . . are, for all practical purposes, insurmountable"

(p. 361). While it is clear that exploring the notion of "experience" philosophically necessitates wading into troubled waters, it will nonetheless be crucial to establish some sense of historical context as well as define the parameters around which I will choose to examine the variations of the concept.

As I explained in the Introduction, here we are most interested in the ways in which a concept of experience has been evoked within a particular expression of educational progressivism—what has come to be called "experiential education." Thus, rather than embarking on an comprehensive philosophical account of experience in education, we will selectively "dip down" into these troubled waters to explore the most salient constructions of experience for this project in both the larger philosophical world as well as the more specific discourses in education. The litmus test for what would be considered important here is threefold. First, we will detail those thinkers from larger philosophical traditions who have been particularly influential in terms of defining and conceptualizing a distinctive construction of experience to experiential education. Second, we will explore those within the field of educational philosophy who, in the words of Martin Jay (2005), "have put 'experience' to greatest work in their thought" (p. 4). Finally, we will discuss those in the modern context who have come to be considered foundational figures in the emerging field of experiential education. It is my hope that dipping down into these three waters of experience will provide the historical and philosophical context to move forward to an engagement with the varieties of experience used in experiential education. As the selection from Dewey that begins this chapter illuminates, the challenge is to organize an understanding of what educational experience signifies. That is the challenge I plan to take up here.

While it may seem somewhat of a cliché to begin with definitions and etymology, it is crucial to establishing and "bounding" this exploration for practical purposes. The most concise and directly relevant exploration of the etymology of experience for this project can be found in Martin Jay's *Songs of Experience* where he details the Latin, Greek, and German origins of the term. In it, he explains how "the English word is understood to be derived most directly from the Latin *experientia*, which denoted 'trial, proof, or experiment'" (2005, p. 10). Curiously, he goes on to note how the verb "to try" in Italian (*expereri*) shares a root with the word for "peril" or "danger" (*periculum*) which suggests a "covert association between experience and peril [and that experience comes] from having survived risks and learned something from the encounter" (p. 10). This will become an important element of modern experiential education theory, as we will discuss later. Jay goes on to discuss the Greek etymology of experience, detailing how the Greek *empeira* serves as the root for the English word "empirical" (p. 10). In describing the significance of such a root, Jay notes (pp. 10–11):

[h]ere a crucial link between experience and raw, unreflected sensation or unmediated observation (as opposed to reason, theory, or speculation) is

already evident. So too is the association between experience as dealing with more specific than general matters, with particulars rather than universals. As such, it contributes to the belief, which we will encounter in certain usages, that experiences are personal and incommunicable, rather than collective and exchangeable.

Finally, Jay devotes special attention to the German equivalents of "experience" (*Erlebnis* and *Erfahrung*) as, to him, they indicate key distinctions for how the term will later be signified. Both *Erlebnis* and *Erfahrung* translate to "experience" in English but mean quite different things. According to Jay, "*Erlebnis* contains within it the root for life (*Leben*) and is sometimes translated as 'lived experience.' . . . Although *Leben* can suggest the entirety of a life, *Erlebnis* generally connotes a more immediate, pre-reflective, and personal variant of experience than *Erfahrung*" (p. 11). By contrast, Jay argues that *Erfahrung* moves beyond immediate and individual notions of experience to a more collective and reflective type of wisdom (p. 11):

> [I]t came to mean a more temporally elongated notion of experience based on a learning process, an integration of discrete moments of experience into a narrative whole or an adventure. This latter view, which is sometimes called a dialectical notion of experience, connotes a progressive, if not always smooth, movement over time, which is implied by the *Fahr* (journey) embedded in *Erfahrung* and the linkage with the German word for danger (*Gefahr*). As such, it activates a link between memory and experience, which subtends the belief that cumulative experience can produce a kind of wisdom that comes only at the end of the day.

As Jay goes on to suggest, these multiple meanings and origins allow for experience to be actualized for any number of philosophical projects, often with contradictory or competing aims. Indeed, this can be seen even at a basic level where "experience" can be employed as a noun (to have "had an experience"), to a verb (to be "experiencing" something in the present), to even "adjectival modifiers such as 'lived,' 'inner,' and 'genuine'" (p. 12).

Thus, if our basic etymological overview suggests anything, it is that attempts to uncover the "true" or "real" root meaning of the term "experience" is surely a foolhardy endeavor. From its very origins, experience has been embedded with various, and often contradictory, meanings and associations. So, for this project, we will ignore Oakeshott's advice to "escape the ambiguities" (Jay, 2005, p. 9) of experience and instead explore the multiple and contested meanings to reveal how they represent different visions of education and, in the end, the good life. Michael Bonnett, in his excellent book *Retrieving Nature: Education for a Post-Humanist Age* discusses the consequences of such an exploration in regards to another ambiguous and contested concept: Nature. His description of the significance of such an exploration provides a salient parallel to our exploration of experience here. Substitute the term "experience" for "nature" below and he aptly describes the implications of such an investigation (2004, pp. 5–6):

> our underlying stance on nature's value will determine how environmental problems will be conceived and the *kinds* of answers that will be sought, that is, what will *count* as an answer. It will thus determine the kinds of knowledge and understanding to be considered relevant, and fundamentally, what the ethical basis for judging policy and action will be.

While there are multiple and contested meanings for experience in education that I will discuss below, it is important to remain aware of the fact that such variety, while it can be celebrated at some level, is not devoid of ethical implications. As Bonnett notes above, there are real consequences to the concepts we employ at the practical level. How we choose to frame and construct experience, to a great extent, defines and determines the kinds of questions and answers we will seek. In this sense, Maslow's famous maxim: "when your only tool is a hammer, every problem begins to look like a nail" applies. We must be cautious and aware of how we frame and construct experience and to what ends, as the consequences of such seemingly "irrelevant" etymology are significant. Indeed, if this were not the case, we would not see the intense passion and conflict generated around such a seemingly innocuous term, both historically and in the modern context. It is those historical constructs that I turn to now.

Historical Roots of Experience in Education

Starting this analysis with the classical period of Western thought certainly has its problems, particularly since the postmodern turn in social theory. Nonetheless, it serves as a good point of departure for several reasons. First, it is well documented that two key figures in the field of experiential education, Kurt Hahn and John Dewey, used and reacted against Greek notions of experience in formulating their own philosophies of experience in education (James, 2008; Jay, 2005). Since these two figures are most commonly cited as "fathers" of experiential education, examining their philosophic predecessors on notions of experience will be important for a richer understanding of their own theoretical and practical projects. Second, the influence of classical Western philosophical thought on present-day orientations to experience and schooling is certainly significant enough to merit close attention. Yet, even given these reasons, it is equally important to be attentive to several important counter-narratives. Various subaltern voices on the role of experience in education need significant attention too. While it is certainly the case in the twenty-first century that notions of experience from women, African-Americans, Native Americans, and other marginalized groups both in the West and in the developing world are rising in attention and prominence, more work needs to be done in exploring the intersections between these so-called marginalized or subaltern voices and present-day experiential education. In this brief historical overview, I will touch on one particular counter-narrative—that of indigenous voices on experience in education—while acknowledging that there are many other histories waiting to be told (this would make an excellent dissertation project for someone by the way). Other voices from the margins will be lifted up as we begin to explore the variations themselves—particularly in terms of feminist notions of experience. For now, while the scope of this chapter and book make it difficult to explore the richness of these historical narratives and counter-narratives in depth, it is worth wading in for a spell.

Early Greek Notions of Experience

The common notion of experience in classical thought is that figures such as Socrates, Plato, and Aristotle tended to emphasize a construction of the term rooted in *empeira* or simple empirical observation (Jay 2005). Often, this characterization is used to contrast the more lowly and basic information that comes from the senses and everyday life to the higher forms of knowledge that can be attained through *theoria*. Following this characterization, the cave story in Plato's *Republic* can be seen as a telling example of how the Platonic worldview pits the ephemeral and deceptive world of the senses against the constant and unchanging light of the forms. Certainly, Dewey takes Plato to task for his denigration of experience. In *Education and Democracy*, Dewey (1916) states in regards to Plato and Aristotle, "[m]uch as these thinkers differed in many respects, they agreed in identifying experience with purely practical concerns; and hence with material interests as to its purpose and with the body as to its organ. Knowledge, on the other hand, existed for its own sake free from practical reference, and found its source and organ in a purely immaterial mind" (p. 262). To Dewey, the Greeks, by dichotomizing the world of material and practical experience from the metaphysical mind started a Western philosophical tradition of "even greater intellectualism" of experience as carried forward by such figures as Locke and Descartes (p. 267).

Yet others (Lloyd, 1991; Jay, 2005) suggest that the early Greek and Latin periods may not have been as hostile and dismissive of experience as Dewey and other scholars may have characterized. Lloyd in particular has suggested that early Greek thought employed a wide variety of attitudes and approaches and cannot be characterized by a single approach or generalization toward experience. In addition, Jay notes that literary evidence of the times suggests considerable popular approval of life beyond the "purely theoretical mind" (p. 15). The popularity of Homer's *Odyssey* and other such epics, including many of the plays at the time, seems to indicate a championing of *Erfahrung* notions of experience. Finally, Jay notes that Greek political and social life appeared to value the active life on a par with the contemplative life through the notion of *"phronesis* or practical wisdom" and that, while *theoria* may have been more emphasized in Aristotle's *Nicomachean Ethics*, it is undeniable that "philosophically, the notion of experience traces back to the Greek thought, especially to Aristotle" (pp. 15–16). Thus, while it seems evident that, on the whole, the Greeks saw a more diminished role for experience epistemologically, a grand narrative that implies classical thought was universally hostile to notions of subjective, lived experience must be troubled. Nonetheless, as Jay himself notes "[t]he legacy of Plato and Aristotle, with varying coherence and often eclectically combined elements on non-Greek thought, dominated medieval philosophy. As a result, the ephemeral happenings of everyday life were rendered marginal in the search for universal truths" (p. 17). So, we might roughly summarize the Greek and classical period contributions to our notions of experience as follows. Through the works of Plato and Aristotle emerged the West's first conceptual notions of experience. While variations and contradictions surely existed, it was evident that the overall approach towards experience during this period was, at best, the notion that experience represented a materially oriented practice towards the achievement of higher theoretical truths (as expressed in the Aristotelian notion of *phronesis*). At worst, experience evoked notions of ephemerality, or of conservatism, custom, and enslavement to the past (as expressed in the Platonic view). These signifiers would have lasting and resonant impressions of notions of experience to come.

Rationalism, Empiricism, and Experience

Picking up most directly and (for the purposes of this survey) relevantly, on this construction of experience was René Descartes (1596–1650). Dewey famously characterized this period as the "quest for certainty" as empiricists such as Descartes, Locke, and Bacon aimed to place Aristotelian experience in "exile" arguing instead for the priority of reason over the senses. Coupled with the Copernican revolution, this dominant epistemology saw the collapse of the Ptolemaic universe as a telling example of the ascendancy of reason. "For Bacon and Descartes . . . the Ptolemaic universe had been disproven, and the geocentric, commonplace 'experience' that had made it plausible was discarded in favor of a truer understanding of the cosmos, one that eagerly moved beyond the finite perspective of the contingent human subject" (Jay, 2005, p. 31). It is difficult to underestimate this shift in worldview. The entire orientation to the universe changed through the Copernican revolution. And, implicated in this shift were the mistakes of personal, subjective "experience" (e.g. watching the sun "revolve" around the earth day after day). What lifted us out of this fundamental error and reoriented our place in the cosmos was a form of empirically derived reason. The Cartesian worldview finally and completely severed the experiencing subject from knowledge acquisition, turning Aristotle's sense-based experience on its head ("I think therefore I am"). To one philosopher of education: "Descartes' philosophy was directed squarely against the Aristotelian philosophy taught in schools of his day. For the Aristotelians, all cognition begins in sensation: everything in the intellect comes first through the senses. Descartes' philosophy, on the other hand, emphasizes the priority of reason over the senses" (Garber, 1998, p. 124). A. D. Laing, for example, argued in regards to this Cartesian mechanization that it "offers us a dead world: Out go sight, sound, taste, touch, and smell, and along with them have since gone esthetic and ethical sensibility, values, quality, soul, consciousness, spirit. *Experience as such is cast out of the realm of scientific discourse*" (quoted in Capra, 1997, p. 19, emphasis added).

This, of course, leads to perhaps the most classic epistemological argument in philosophy between Rationalists, such as Descartes, who disparage the subjectivity of the senses, and Empiricists, such as Hume, who felt that sense data yielded higher truths and that knowledge gained by purely mental means was ungrounded and suspect (Crosby, 1981, p. 8). It was Immanuel Kant (1724–1804) who offered a way out of this epistemological impasse. Kant did not see the mind, as constructed by Descartes and others, as a substance but rather as an activity. By placing the mind as an active subject, Kant could answer both of the problems associated with strict rationalism and strict empiricism. Jay (2005) writes that "Kant . . . boldly sought an answer by focusing less on the object of knowledge than the subject, a constitutive subject that was far more than the succession of its perceptions or site of habitual repetition" (p. 69). In essence, the mind actively organizes and orders the world through perceiving it. Experience, then, helps us yield not a "correspondence notion of truth" but a "coherence model instead" (p. 74). As Crosby (1981) states (p. 10):

> By seeing the mind as the active source of order, rather than some objective unchanging Reality as the order, Kant attempted to solve the problem of certainty. Certainty, Reality, objectivity, etc., all have less-rigorous meanings, in a sense. They are reality-for-us, or objectivity-for-us, but that is good enough. Thanks to Kant, Western thought got beyond this epistemological impasse . . . His theory provides room for both reason and experience to function, and gets us out of the disastrous problem of how to get in touch with that which we want to know.

To reiterate, it is well beyond the scope of this review to explore the varieties and permutations of experience in Western philosophical thought or the debate between the Rationalists and Empiricists in any depth. Nonetheless, the general characteristics of these debates will prove influential to later constructions of experience by those who are evoked more consistently in the field of experiential education (namely Dewey). It was Dewey in particular who picked back up on a notion of experience to try and heal the cleavages brought about by past philosophical approaches to experience that limited and reduced its construction to cognition, abstraction, and the intellect. As Crosby (1981) states, "Dewey saw the need to achieve *certainty* led Western thought to theoretical constructs like those of Plato and Descartes, or to the epistemological impoverishment of Hume. Dewey saw clearly enough to see that the goal of certainty must be rejected as a starting point" (p. 11). We will discuss and explore Dewey's philosophy of experience in much more detail in Chapter 4.

A perceptive reader may notice another glaring omission in the early history we have been exploring—that of Jean-Jacques Rousseau (1712–1778). A contemporary of Kant, Rousseau is perhaps most important to our survey here for his classic work *Emile*, which illuminates his philosophy of education. While Rousseau wrote during the Enlightenment, he is often considered a part of the Romantic period owing to the tremendous influence of his works on that later period. Because of this, we will explore Rousseau's contributions to our notions of experience in the next chapter on Romanticism and experience. For now, we will conclude this chapter by considering a counter-narrative to this brief history of the concept of experience.

Alternative Histories

The few attempts at historical and/or theoretical explorations of experiential education (Fenwick, 2001; Hunt, 1995; Warren et al., 2008) have traced similar terrain to the landscape just mapped above. While it is undeniable that the dominant constructions of experiential education emerge from a Western worldview, it is also important to acknowledge the ways in which such histories have functioned to marginalize other, important ways of knowing about the concept of experience in education. History, after all, is not simply the retelling of "facts about the world." It is a conscious framing, organization, and reconstruction of those facts. History tells stories, stories that generate meanings and frames of reference for us. How we tell those stories, what parts we emphasize, what parts we leave out, speaks volumes about our own ideals, values, and assumptions about the subject at hand. This project is no different. One telling of the intellectual history of experience is to recall the contributions of the "Great White Males" and declare the project complete. But this is certainly not the whole of the story. But where do we go from here? Separating other, marginalized voices out into their own chapter is problematic in the sense that it suggests some "essential" characteristics of, say, Eastern philosophical thought while ignoring the variations and complexity within these notions of experience. Furthermore, a chapter (or section of a chapter) on marginalized identities and their notions of experience smacks of tokenism. Such a framework just seems to reproduce existing inequalities and legitimize racialized histories. As Patricia Hill Collins (2000) noted (p. 15):

> Race, class, and gender still constitute intersecting oppressions, but the ways in which they are now organized to produce social injustice differ from

prior eras. Just as theories, epistemologies, and facts produced by any group of individuals represent the standpoints and interests of their creators, the very definition of who is legitimated to do intellectual work is not only politically contested, but is changing ... Reclaiming Black feminist intellectual traditions involves much more than developing Black feminist analyses using standard epistemological criteria. It also involves challenging the very terms of intellectual discourse itself.

Taken to its fullest extent, bringing voices in from the outside means changing the foundational assumptions about what "counts" as intellectual history and what we value in contemporary scholarship. Is Dewey, for example, important because of some objective criteria in regards to the intellectual weight of his ideas or is he important because we made him so? In making him important, whose work did we ignore or under-appreciate? By repeatedly citing him, are we functionally reproducing existing inequalities, over-emphasizing the intellectual importance of the West? Of Whites? Of men? How far down the rabbit hole do we choose to go? Perhaps the best that we can do here is agree with the statement that figures like Plato, Descartes, Kant, and Dewey are important "because we made them so." And, this is enough to make them worthy of investigation. What we cannot do, should not do, is simply stop the conversation there. The concept of a counter-narrative speaks to the importance of interrupting the dominant story and offering alternatives. Counter-narratives need not be comprehensive. They need only to challenge us to question taken-for-granted assumptions, worldviews, and orientations. They serve to illustrate by example. To return to our river metaphor, counter-currents are always worth paying attention to. They create the eddies, boundaries, and other transition zones where life often thrives. Life is always more interesting at the margins. As a fisherman, I know that often the biggest fish lie in these zones. Ignore the counter-current, as a boater, and you may find yourself upside down in your kayak, or out of your raft going for a ride down the rapids. While there are many possible counter-narratives worth exploring here, we will focus here on one—that of indigenous constructions of experience in education, in the hopes that it serves to question some of the taken-for-granted perspectives inherent in the narrative just considered.

Indigenous Constructions of Experience and Education

Here again, we tread into dangerous water by lifting up some generalized and universal expression of experience employed by "indigenous peoples." Indeed, the cultural appropriation of native peoples in experiential and environmental education has been previously critiqued (Oles in Warren et al., 1995). There is certainly no one universal way of knowing that can rightly be called "indige-nous." As Linda Tuhiwai Smith (2005) points out: "native communities are not homogenous, [they] do not agree on the same issues, and do not live in splendid isolation from the world" (p. 87). Even in the North American context, claiming one "Native American" way of knowing ignores the complexity and variation present in tribal identities and cultures. As Gary Nabhan (1997) notes in regards to Indian communities in the United States (p. 91):

> Despite such diversity within and between North American cultures, it is quite common to read statements implying a uniform "American Indian view of nature"—as if all the diverse cultural relations with particular habitats on the continent can be swept under an all-encompassing rug . . . This assumption is both erroneous and counter-productive in that it undermines any respect for cultural diversity. It does not grant cultures— indigenous or otherwise—the capacity to evolve, to diverge from one another, to learn about their local environments through time.

Such generalizations can lead to a certain romanticization of indigenous peoples as the "ecologically noble savage" (Hames, 2007). Denevan (1998), for example, has shown that Indian peoples in North America did not live in harmony with a "pristine wilderness" prior to the arrival of White Europeans. Bowers (1997) states: "It needs to be kept in mind, for example, that not all traditional cultures are models of ecological citizenship. Nor should all low-status forms of know-ledge that underlie cultural practices of marginalized groups be considered immune from criticism and reform efforts" (p. 10). But the romanticized notions of the indigene go beyond the "noble savage" to a construction of the "native" as spiritually superior and as more "naturally" inclined to learn through experi-ence. These particular frames of reference are not innocent. As Smith (2005) argues "[t]he desire for 'pure,' uncontaminated, and simple definitions of the native by the settler is often a desire to continue to know and define the Other" (p. 86). These concerns in regards to the romanticization of indigenous cultures and ways of knowing are real and must be addressed in order to develop a more well-rounded discussion of indigenous ways of knowing. There is a fine line between using indigenous ways of knowing as a form of cultural critique and the appropriation and (mis)representation of cultural traditions to further neo-colonialist projects.

Indigenous Knowledge Systems

Nonetheless, it seems equally egregious to *deny* that there may be indigenous ways of knowing that represent clear and compelling counter-narratives to dominant, Enlightenment-oriented epistemologies. Gary Nabhan (1995), Keith Basso (1996), Linda Tuhiwai Smith (2005), Winona LaDuke (1999), and David Abram (1997), for example, have offered compelling examples and cases of distinct worldviews and knowledge systems expressed in native peoples. Bowers (1997) notes, for example, that "understanding the complexity of local knowledge, as well as the ability of indigenous cultures to avoid the modern mistake of commodifying nature and naturalizing . . . scientific approaches . . . provides an important vantage point for recognizing the aspects of modern consciousness that are largely taken for granted" (p. 98). Basso, in *Wisdom Sits in Places*, contends that the Apache notion of wisdom offers a clear alternative to Western ways of knowing (1996, p. 146):

> [F]eatures of the Apache landscape, their richly evocative names, and the many tribal narratives that recall their mythic importance are viewed as resources with which determined men and women can modify aspects of themselves, including, most basically their own ways of thinking . . . As Apache men and women set about drinking from places—as they acquire knowledge of their natural surroundings, commit it to permanent memory, and apply it productively to the workings of their minds—they show by their actions that their surroundings live in them.

To Basso, how the Apache "drink from places" and allow places to work on them and live in them gives them a way of knowing that is distinctive and counter to dominant Western epistemologies. Well beyond constructions of the ecologically Noble Savage, Basso's detailed ethnographic account of Western Apache landscape and language reminds us that we can speak of indigenous ways of knowing as a counter-narrative without resorting to tokenism, stereotyping, or romanticization.

Many scholars, from a variety of disciplines, have written about the distinctive features of indigenous knowledge systems that set them apart from Western, Enlightenment-oriented epistemologies. Barnhardt (2008) for example, notes that "[although] Western science and education tend to emphasize compartmentalized knowledge that is often decontextualized and taught in the detached setting of a classroom or laboratory, Indigenous people have traditionally acquired their knowledge through direct experience in the natural environment" (p. 11). Basso (1996) argues that "Apache conceptions of wisdom differ markedly from those contained in Western ideologies" (p. 130) and goes on to say that "[t]his view of mental development rests on the premise that knowledge is useful to the extent that it can be swiftly recalled and turned without effort to practical ends" (p. 134). Gary Nabhan commented, in regards to the valuation of indigenous knowledge of the natural world—what is often referred to as "ethnoecology"—that "[i]f . . . this 'folk knowledge' is categorically dismissed as unscientific and ultimately replaced by Western scientific knowledge alone, we stand to lose something of import" (2003, p. 3). Finally, it is worth noting the record of success (or lack thereof) of many indigenous peoples in Western-styled schooling. As many have argued (Adams, 1997; Delpit, 1995; Wolcott, 1997), this resistance to conventional schooling is not the result of some lack of intelligence or cultural deficit; rather, it indicates the cultural conflict clearly apparent in radically different approaches to education and learning. Clearly, indigenous ways of knowing have the potential to offer counter-narratives to the history of experience in education described previously. So, what then can we say about notions of experience and education from indigenous worldviews?

Experiential Education from Indigenous Perspectives

The construction of experience apparent in many forms of traditional or "native" schooling present several distinct differences from the Western history outlined previously. We can't begin to survey even a small percentage of the diversity and depth of these worldviews. As a result, a single illustrative example will have to suffice. The case of Charles Eastman (1858–1939) offers us a window into how these educational approaches can be set against Western ways of connecting experience and learning. Eastman (Ohiyesa), a Santee Sioux who grew up in Minnesota, wrote several books and articles including covering his boyhood and schooling years. In *From the Deep Woods to Civilization* (1916), Eastman noted that "it is commonly supposed that there is no systematic education of their children among the aborigines of this country. Nothing could be further from the truth" (1916/1977, p. 41). Eastman's stories and tales of growing up Sioux describe a boyhood that is at the same time harsh, playful, and full of meaning. Dorothy Lee, in *Valuing the Self* (1986), recounts a story in another Eastman text, *Indian Boyhood* (1902). It is worth quoting at length as it aptly describes one form of an indigenous approach to experiential education.

> When he was five or six, he took off in the early morning. No one sent him out, no one told him where to go, or what places to avoid; no one told him when to get back, or what to do if he got tired or bored . . . This was his own choice. His uncle, who was taking the place of father, said to him: "Look closely to everything you see." Only this. The boy went forth, perhaps joining his friends, perhaps wandering all day alone. When he returned in the evening his uncle was there waiting for him with questions . . . "On what side of the trees is the lighter colored bark?" The boy had not been told to look for this. But he had been admonished to look closely, and he had done so. He can answer. The uncle listens closely and asks more questions. The boy describes the birds he has seen, their color, the shape of their bills, their song . . . He ventures a name; but this is only a guess. It is not for him to name; this depends on the language of the community. So the uncle corrects him and gives him the "proper" name.
>
> *Lee, 1986, pp. 35–36*

This vignette reveals several distinguishing factors of indigenous ways of knowing as connected to experiential education. As Barnhardt (2008) notes, "traditional" or "native" knowledge systems tend to emphasize the importance of a holistic approach to learning. As the Eastman account reveals, the boy's education is not compartmentalized into separate subject matter and disciplines, but, rather, through the experiences and observations of his day, he is asked to see the connections between things. It is decidedly practical and relational, based on careful observation, experimentation, and local, as opposed to global, verification (Barnhardt 2008). In addition, there is a trust in "inherited wisdom" (p. 16). Eastman does not simply "individualize" his learning through independent study of the natural world, he checks his own understanding with his uncle at the end of the day. This connection to the larger community and his elders illustrates the vital importance of oral history and the adage that "it takes a village to raise a child." As Lee describes, "He ventures a name; but this is only a guess. It is not for him to name; this depends on the language of the community. So the uncle corrects him and gives him the 'proper' name" (1986, p. 36). Finally, experience here is deeply contextual and place-based. It becomes weighted, it means something, only through its location in a particular place. It is specific, not generalizable. And, it is constant, not special. As Basso (1996) notes about Apache notions of experience and place (p. 144):

> A variety of experience, sense of place also represents a culling of experience. It is what has accrued—and never stops accruing—from lives spent sensing places . . . As such, it is greeted as natural, normal, and despite the ambivalent feelings it sometimes produces, entirely unremarkable. Experience delivered neat (though not, as I say, always very neatly), sense of place is accepted as a simple fact of life, as a regular aspect of how things are.

As we shall see, this idea of experience as place-based *and* everyday in orientation is in stark contrast to the more Romantic (and sublime) constructions of experience we will explore in the next chapter.

Experience still teaches here, just as it did for the Greeks and Enlightenment thinkers. But this vignette reveals the way indigenous knowledge systems can view learning as deeply contextual and integrated. The wisdom (*Erfahrung*) of the elders is trusted and not viewed with the sort of skepticism embedded within the standard Western scientific method. Experience becomes something not rationally tested but rather woven into metaphor, story, and oral tradition. It ties together the physical and metaphysical realms and, as a result, allows for the possibility of expanding beyond an anthropocentric worldview. Experience, once decoupled from a rational, autonomous self, becomes something that connects across and between not only human subjects but also other subjects including both animate and, even, inanimate objects. David Abram (1997) in *The Spell of the Sensuous*, describes how Western researchers have managed to overlook how magic is not just a supernatural practice to a Balinese shaman but a deeply natural and ecological practice as well. To Abram, this oversight reveals the ways in which

Western notions of knowledge and experience are viewed as determinate and mechanical. To Abram (pp. 9–10, emphasis in text):

> Magic, then, in its perhaps most primordial sense, is the experience of existing in a world made up of multiple intelligences, the intuition that every form one perceives—from the swallow swooping overhead to the fly on a blade of grass, and indeed the blade of grass itself—is an *experiencing* form, an entity with its own predilections and sensations, albeit sensations that are very different than our own.

Winona LaDuke (1999) describes the Seminole worldview in a similar fashion: "Where the natural world ends and the human world begins, there you will find the Seminoles. There is no distinction between the two worlds—the Creator's Law governs all" (p. 27).

While there is much more we might say about indigenous approaches to learning and its connection with experiential education, for the purposes of this brief survey we are left with the following observations. While caution is advised in terms of generalizing and/or romanticizing "native" ways of knowing and learning, indigenous knowledge systems can represent important counter-narratives to the ways in which the notion of experience in learning is constructed. They question how Western notions of experience in education are often set up as mechanical and deterministic. They offer different notions of validity and verification based upon experience as accumulated wisdom in particular places. They illustrate a construction of experience not individually located but rather intersubjectively connected—both in and between other humans but extending out beyond that to other experiencing subjects while connecting the natural and supernatural realms. Each of these observations suggests that limiting our brief narrative history of experience in education to Western Enlightenment-oriented epistemologies would be a mistake. They also suggest that fertile ground exists to explore many more counter-narratives to continue to expand (and trouble) our historical understanding of the intellectual roots of experience and experiential education.

Conclusion

This brief survey of the most prominent voices on experience in education in the premodern period sets up several over-arching themes for the remainder of this project. First, from the etymology of the word "experience," we find that any hope of consensus as to the "true" root meaning of the word must be abandoned. Almost written in to the very structure of the term is contestation and dissent. From the split between the German *Erlebnis* and *Erfahrung* we can see that experience has never been a homogeneous or "*Ur*" concept. This variation is reinforced by a cursory survey of major Western thinkers on the notion and, indeed, cuts to the heart of the classic philosophical debate between rationalism and empiricism. Is experience an individual and subjective force that cannot be trusted? Or, rather, does it form the very core of humankind's search for generalizable knowledge and wisdom? Certainly Kant advanced philosophical thought beyond this most basic impasse. Yet, the tensions between notions of *Erlebnis* and *Erfahrung* remain.

Finally, our counter-narrative example of indigenous knowledge systems suggests the need for a re-examination of taken-for-granted assumptions about certain notions of experience and learning. Is the experiencing subject autonomous? How might we think about experience differently if it is decoupled from the individual subject? How pervasive is the Western scientific method in our ways of thinking about experience and learning? How do we expand our notions of experience beyond the rational to the supernatural and the magical? Can we? Should we? These challenges to certain Enlightenment-oriented epistemological traditions will resonate in our next chapter where we will consider Romantic notions of experience in education. Our counter-narrative also reminds us of the crucial importance of the subaltern voice, and that we must throughout this journey be attentive to the story we are telling, the frames we are using, and what we are choosing to exclude. As the Dewey quotation at the beginning of the chapter reminds us, the challenge is to understand what educational experience signifies. If there is one thing we are left with at the conclusion of this brief historical overview, it is the realization that this river of experience is *already* complex and full of contradictions at its intellectual headwaters.

3

EXPERIENCE AND THE INDIVIDUAL

The Romantic Current

I stand in awe of my body, this matter to which I am bound has become
so strange to me. I fear not spirits, ghosts, of which I am one—that my body
might—but I fear bodies, I tremble to meet them. What is this Titan that
has taken possession of me? Talk of mysteries—Think of our life in
nature—daily to be shown matter, to come in contact with it—rocks, trees,
wind on our cheeks! the solid earth! the actual world! the common sense!
Contact! Contact! Who are we? Where are we?

Henry David Thoreau

Introduction

As this chapter begins in earnest the exploration of the core theoretical currents
in our river of experience, it will be worth saying something about how these
chapters will be organized. As I discussed in the Introduction, the four currents
explored next—Experience and the Individual; Experience and the Social;
Experience and the Political, and Experience and the Market—comprise the main
theoretical influences on how we construct curriculum projects in experiential
education today. While there is some degree of rough chronology to the way
they are ordered, all four currents are clearly in evidence today and so this
organizing framework should not really be seen as historical or teleological. In
each chapter, we will first discuss the general context from which the "worldview" of each of these currents emerges before settling into a specific discussion
of the main characteristics of the current and the ways in which they influence
our notions of experience in education. Each chapter will conclude with some
discussion of the "possibilities and limitations" of the theoretical current in terms
of present-day curriculum projects and theorizing. It is not my intent here to be

the judge and jury of which current is "right" or "wrong" in its construction of experience. As I noted in the Introduction, we are most interested in how experience has been put to use and what the consequences of such usages are. As such, I am using the frame of "possibilities and limitations" in the hopes that readers take *both* an empathetic *and* a critical read to notions of experience in each current.

Needless to say, as I mentioned in our previous chapter, there is considerable danger in "skimming the surface" of some very complex theoretical histories as I will aim to do here. Generalizations will most certainly be made. But, I take comfort in something Isaiah Berlin once wrote: "unless we do use some generalizations it is impossible to trace the course of human history" (1999, p. 20). I am certainly not claiming here to trace the course of human history; the concept of experience in education is plenty big enough thank you. Nevertheless, the point is a good one. We are most interested in these next four chapters in the "big ideas" and, as such, we'll talk about some "big" social and intellectual movements and histories including Romanticism, progressivism, and critical theory. Works on each of these alone could fill several large libraries and I would encourage curious and interested readers to dive into the deeper pools of the currents that you find most intriguing. My hope here is to get the big ideas more or less right. It's a big river and there is a lot to cover.

In this chapter, we'll begin first by exploring the historical roots of a more individualized notion of educative experience as it emerges in the Romantic period. We'll identify several key characteristics of "Romantic experience" and then explore how these have carried forth into contemporary theorizing in experiential education. Moving beyond Romanticism, we'll briefly examine how this particular construction intersects with notions of education within existentialism. We'll conclude by illustrating several examples of visible curriculum projects that might employ this version of experience and explore the limitations inherent in the current.

Romanticism and Experience

As with our exploration of the term "experience," we run into similar tricky terrain in attempting to legislate a single accepted use of a term such as "Romanticism." Isaiah Berlin (1999) describes it as a "dangerous and confused subject, in which many have lost, I will not say their senses, but at any rate their sense of direction" (p. 1). Various writers have described the mood, movement, or ideals of the Romantic period in vastly different, and sometimes contradictory, ways. Yet Berlin also goes on to argue that "there *was* a romantic movement; it did have something which was central to it; it did create a revolution in consciousness; and it is important to discover what this is" (emphasis in text, p. 20). Indeed, it is somewhat surprising that, given the influence of Romanticism on Western thought, its influence has remained more or less unexplored in the field of experiential education. This despite the fact that key figures in the history of the field, figures such as Henry David Thoreau, John Muir, Maria Montessori, and John Dewey clearly draw inspiration from Romantic sensibilities. Indeed, as I will attempt to demonstrate in this chapter, one could make a strong argument that it is in Romanticism that we find the single strongest theoretical current in our exploration of experiential education. It is for this reason that it is worth wandering in, despite the obvious perils.

While it comprises a complex and varied intellectual, political, and artistic period, Romanticism can be broadly characterized as a "nineteenth century movement of reaction against the values, tastes, and ideas of the preceding century" (Hay, 2002, p. 4). The preceding century was, of course, the "Age of Enlightenment" and represented a distinctive set of intellectual norms and views from which the Romantics took issue. In particular, the Enlightenment's emphasis on a particular kind of objectivist-oriented science and the ascendance of human reason as the highest form of intellectual progress brought about a passionate reaction from those who saw the social dislocation from the industrial revolution and the subsequent ills of society and "civilization" pitted against the "common" and "natural man." The Romantic temperament placed higher value on the eccentricities of the individual, the role of emotion and sentiment in life and learning, the exotic over the familiar, and held a deeply skeptical view of modernity and the role reason played in definitions of "progress" and the good life. But such general characterizations can be taken too far. Pitting reason against emotion, realism against imagination, and science against nature implies a too-easy dichotomy between Enlightenment and Romantic ideals. The reality is a much more interwoven relationship between a complex cluster of ideas in philosophy, political thought, and arts and letters. Nonetheless, Romanticism *did* set in motion the first critique of modernity and many of the ideals of the Enlightenment. And, in particular, the influence of Romanticism on one social institution—education—is of particular interest for our exploration in this chapter. We will examine two main influences to our notions of experience in education. First, through the ideas of Jean-Jacques Rousseau and his classic educational treatise, *Emile*, we will look at how Romantic notions of individuality and learning intersect with our notions of experience in education. Second, through exploring the ideas of the Romantic Transcendentalists such as Emerson, Thoreau, and Muir, we will see how constructions of nature and, in particular, learning-in-nature, bring about a distinctive current in the field of experiential education.

Enlightenment views on Education

Prior to Rousseau, the dominant Enlightenment-oriented approach to education was "classicist" in the sense that it emphasized the values of order, discipline, and intellectual rigor, favoring Apollonian rationality over Dionysian impulses and emotionalism. The belief in the power of reason brought about a certain skepticism of base human nature, instinct, and emotion. Children in this worldview were not necessarily inclined toward the good from birth. In fact, the "primitivism" and emotionalism of childhood was looked down upon as it was only in the development of the capacities to reason that individuals truly lived out their human potential. Freedom, in the classicism of the Enlightenment era, was realized not in the individual following his or her passions and bliss but in the careful study and acquisition of time-tested knowledge and the development of rigorous intellectual capabilities. Thomas Jefferson, for example, was enormously influenced by Enlightenment thought and believed freedom from tyranny came about through education and the cultivation of a meritocracy. The greatest danger to a democracy, in Jefferson's view, was an uneducated populace and it was the reason he fought so hard to pass his Bill for a More General Diffusion of Knowledge (1778) in the Virginia state assembly. In his view, a population that followed every whim and bliss would make it all the more vulnerable to manipulation, propaganda, and, eventually, tyrannical governance. To Jefferson, education was important as it would:

> qualify [students] as judges of the actions and designs of men; it will enable them to know the ambition under every disguise it may assume; and knowing how to defeat its views. In every government on earth is some trace of human weakness, some germ of corruption and degeneracy, which cunning will discover, and wickedness insensibly open, cultivate, and improve.
>
> The Life and Selected Writings of Thomas Jefferson, *p. 265*

The emphasis here on human weakness and degeneracy points the reader to the notion that, for Enlightenment thinkers and those like Jefferson who were profoundly influenced by this worldview, human nature was not necessarily inclined toward the good. In fact, left to their own devices, instincts, and impulses, individuals were not really to be trusted at all. As Berlin (1999) argues, the Enlightenment worldview held that "[t]here is only one way of discovering . . . answers, and that is by the correct use of reason, deductively as in the mathematical sciences, inductively as in the sciences of nature. That is the only way in which answers in general—true answers to serious questions—may be obtained" (p. 22). Thus, the general stance toward education during the eighteenth century viewed ideas such as the innate goodness of children, impulses, emotions, and "gut instincts" with skepticism and a fair amount of distrust. These were phenomena outside the realm of reason and the rationality of the scientific method. They could not be used to answer "serious questions." Again, for Berlin (p. 21):

> If the answer is not knowable at all, if the answer is in some way in principle shrouded from us, then there must be something wrong with the question.

This is the proposition which is common both to Christians and to scholastics, to the Enlightenment and to the positivist tradition of the twentieth century. It is, in fact, the backbone of the main Western tradition, and it is this that romanticism cracked.

In stark contrast to this worldview, Rousseau's *Emile* presages the cracking of the backbone Berlin describes above. Just as importantly for our specific purposes here, it sets the stage for the emergence of a very particular notion of the role of experience in education.

Rousseau's *Emile*

In *Emile* (1762), Rousseau lays out his educational and schooling ideal—one that examines the relationship between the individual and society and represented a direct challenge to state-sponsored notions of schooling. While Rousseau was, technically, an Enlightenment thinker by time period, he is considered to be an early Romantic—particularly with *Emile*. Rousseau considered *Emile* "the best and most important of my writings" (1953, pp. 529–30) and it was so controversial that many early copies were burned. In it, Rousseau described the ideal educational process for the natural man he argues for in *The Social Contract* (1762) through his central characters, Emile and his Tutor. The first and most famous sentence, "Everything is good as it leaves the hands of the Author of things; everything degenerates in the hands of man," sets the stage for what Rousseau viewed as the corrupting influences of society on the innate goodness of the child. In stark contrast to Enlightenment- and classicist-oriented views on schooling, the education of Emile is decidedly individual and experiential in order to free the child from the corrupting influences of society. As A. Rorty (1998) argues (p. 248):

> *Emile* is in many ways like natural man, and it is the Tutor's task to keep him that way as long as possible. He is independent and active . . . He is to learn from experience, by the consequences of his actions rather than from persons or books. If he were taught by the Tutor, the complex relations of power and dependence would be set in motion . . . When he learns from experience, he remains free and active.

The student who is described in Rousseau's *Emile* is, in many ways, the proto-typical experiential student. Freed from the confines of didactic and "artificial" instruction, he learns by following his interests and through his experiences in the world. Rousseau frames this purposefully as a more "natural" form of learning, one that is set against the artificial and corrupting form of development that occurs in association with society.

In *Emile*, Rousseau sets the educational stage whereby the experiencing individual is capable of learning in a "natural" state protected, in essence, from the "complex relations of power and dependence" (A. Rorty, 1998, p. 248) of the State. Contrast this with Jefferson's vision described earlier. To Jefferson, the individual was *more free* the more he engaged in the intellectual history of the world, reading classic texts, learning from experts, and developing his character and sense of citizenship through State-sponsored schooling. This socialization process protected the individual from the tyranny of the State by cultivating the capacity to think and reason for oneself. For Rousseau, it was almost the exact opposite. Only by freeing Emile from the weight of the preconceived and corrupt intellectual histories of the past was his student more likely to live free. The child, to Rousseau, is born "free" and it is only through the socialization process that he finds himself in chains. This, by the way, does not mean Jefferson and Rousseau did not agree on other important matters. If we are not careful, we could take this distinction too far. Both men had the same end in mind—independent thought and freedom from tyranny; it was the means to that end where they differed on matters of education. Indeed, indicative of their shared concerns beyond education, Rousseau's *Social Contract* was one of the most influential works for the Founding Fathers in the development of the Declaration of Independence and Constitution of the United States. Nonetheless, the distinctions here matter. While both Jefferson and Rousseau viewed education as a means of protecting the individual from the tyranny of the State, each had differing means to that end. In Jefferson we see the embodiment of Enlightenment-oriented classicist thinking on education. In Rousseau's *Emile*, we see the beginnings of a very different approach to education—one that placed experience at the center of the learning endeavor.

After *Emile*, Johann Pestalozzi (1746–1827) was perhaps the most well known in attempting to put Rousseau's educational theories into practice. Pestalozzi, a Swiss politician and social activist, turned his attention to education in later years, becoming famous and widely read across Europe for his distinctive schooling approaches, even advising Napoleon on creating a national education system in France. What became known as the "Pestalozzi Method" was a practical approach to education drawing from Rousseau's sense of teaching toward "human nature." Pestalozzi's method emphasized the child's innate curiosities and spontaneity, insisting that the child not be told what to do but, rather, that she figure it out for herself. William Kilpatrick (1951), a later progressive educator who was a student of John Dewey, described Pestalozzi's doctrine of *Anschauung*—or, the belief in the importance of direct experience (pp. viii–ix):

> No word was to be used for any purpose until adequate *Anschauung* had preceded. The thing or distinction must be felt or observed in the concrete. Pestalozzi's followers developed various sayings from this: from the known to the unknown, from the simple to the complex, from the concrete to the abstract.

Here again we see the importance of the direct experience for the child. By emphasizing an educational flow from the "known to the unknown" and the "concrete to the abstract" Pestalozzi takes Rousseau's *Emile* and gives it a more specific methodological thrust and purpose. Children must actively sense and feel their immediate surroundings and it is the educator's job to provide the freedom necessary for the child to follow his or her natural inclinations. Rousseau, Pestalozzi, and others in the European Romantic movement of the late eighteenth century codified what could appropriately be called a Romantic stance on education—one that was, in many respects, a precursor to the progressive educational movement of the late nineteenth and early twentieth centuries. E. D. Hirsch (1996) summarizes this worldview (p. 74):

> First, Romanticism believed that human nature is innately good, and should therefore be encouraged to take its natural course, unspoiled by the artificial impositions of social prejudice and convention. Second, Romanticism concluded that the child is neither a scaled-down, ignorant version of the adult nor a formless piece of clay in need of molding, rather, the child is a special being in its own right with unique, trustworthy—indeed holy— impulses that should be allowed to develop and run their course.

Building from this foundation, a particular form of Romanticism, American Romantic Transcendentalism, would amplify this notion of natural, experiential learning by shifting the ideal from "natural state" and "natural man" to "Nature." This shift, and the subsequent privileging and coupling of Nature and experience would create a highly influential intellectual tradition that continues to resonate today in the discourses on experiential education. And it is this tradition that we turn to presently.

Experience and Nature: Romantic Transcendentalism

In 1865, the American poet Walt Whitman took pen to paper and wrote the following poem, titled "When I Heard the Learn'd Astronomer":

> When I heard the learn'd astronomer;
> When the proofs, the figures, were ranged in columns before me;
> When I was shown the charts and the diagrams, to add, divide, and measure
>   them;
> When I, sitting, heard the astronomer, where he lectured with much
>   applause in the lecture room,
> How soon, unaccountable, I became tired and sick;
> Till rising and gliding out, I wander'd off by myself,
> In the mystical moist night-air, and from time to time,
> Look'd up in perfect silence at the stars.
>
> *Whitman,* Leaves of Grass

Here we see many of the elements that connect Rousseau's vision in *Emile* with the Romantic Transcendentalists of the nineteenth century in the United States. With *Emile*, experience becomes particularly valorized and set against other socializing forces as a form of freeing activity. Rousseau becomes one of the first to connect this idea of "learning by doing" to a transformational process—one that pits education in the broadest sense against schooling as organized by society. In Whitman's poem, the speaker rejects the "proofs," "charts," and "lectures" of the "learn'd astronomer" for the "perfect silence" of the stars. It is clear from the speaker's perspective that he gets much more from his solitary walk than he does from the formal lecturing of the expert. In *Emile*, it is the individual exploration and experience that forms the educative good life. And, such freedom is contrasted with the constraints of the social realm—that of civilization, and the corrupting influences of society. In Whitman's poem, the speaker becomes "sick" and "tired" and then "rises" and wanders off by himself into the "mystical moist night-air." To Whitman, the social gathering of the lecture hall is degenerative and it is only when he physically "rises" and moves outside into Nature that he finds a degree of freedom and regeneration. This dichotomization between Nature (as freeing and transformative) on the one hand and Culture (as corrupting and constraining) on the other, is a central feature of the Romantic Transcendental movement in the United States.

Typically identified by the period around the 1830s in the United States and through the works of Ralph Waldo Emerson, Henry David Thoreau, and John Muir, the Romantic Transcendental movement brought the concept of Nature into particular focus and, in the process, coupled a particular notion of experience with it. This line of thinking begins in earnest with Emerson. As Hay (2002) recounts (p. 7):

> Emerson expounds the notion that a higher "Reason" of intuitive insight, through which it is possible to attain oneness with God and God's natural creation, is the path to true understanding, rather than the deduction from history and science urged by philosophers of the Enlightenment . . . there is a notion that nature is an aspect of God—to study nature in her concrete manifestations is, therefore, to know God and his creation.

Rather than the deductive reason espoused by the Enlightenment, Emerson argued for the inductive process illustrated by *Emile* and then gave that process a particular context—Nature. No longer do the cathedrals and buildings of society bring us closer to God, it is the mountain-top that serves as cathedral, and experiences-in-Nature that serve as our form of worship. And, through this process we are "saved"—both individually and collectively as a society.

This notion of the redemptive and "innocent" quality of Nature is picked up by Henry David Thoreau and John Muir where it was given a particular focus: wilderness preservation. For Thoreau and Muir, "Nature" became embodied within a particular ideal: "wilderness." As they witnessed the closing of the Eastern frontier and the demise of large tracks of forest, the dichotomy between Nature and Civilization took on a certain concreteness that placed their philosophical leanings in stark relief. The vitality of Nature, embodied through untrammeled wilderness and wild spaces, was under direct threat by an advancing civilization carrying with it a whole host of negative attributes. Pollution, deforestation, industrialization, social unrest, and overcrowding represented, to many in the Romantic Transcendental movement, "old Europe" and its problems while the American West, with its wilderness, "empty space," and unrealized possibilities represented America's ability to continue to define itself by the frontier, and by moving away, physically and metaphorically, from Europe. For Thoreau and Muir, wilderness and wilderness preservation became the embodiment of social reform. According to these early environmentalists, direct experience with Nature happens most readily in wilderness and, by association, the disappearance of wilderness signaled the disappearance of the opportunity for liberating and transcendent experience (and thus, by extension, social reform).

If nature and civilization are set against one another, and the path to liberation and transformation is tied directly to wilderness and wildness,[1] then it follows that knowledge is attained by the individual embodiment of experience in such settings. This was, in essence, an epistemological claim. Experience, and thus knowledge, becomes individually lived from this perspective. Thoreau's quote at the beginning of this chapter illustrates this stance. His famous exhortation as he climbs Mount Katahdin in Maine of "Contact! Contact!" reveals his belief in direct experience-in-Nature as a sublime and transcendent phenomenon. As David Rothenberg (2002) argued (p. 46):

> Thoreau realizes on the climb up Katahdin that he treads upon an earth that was not made for him or his ilk, a land of Titans, the clouded tablelands of sublimity above the cliff falling down to the timid plains of humanity . . . And yet there is a need for the visit, the place serves a purpose, and affects him. He is leaping past the veil of explanation, and the Earth is touching him. "Contact!" he implores, as the stark country makes a deep impression upon him. It is the country for philosophy. We need raw wildness in order to learn how to think.

---

1   There is a significant body of writing within the environmental genre that examines the differences between notions of "wilderness" and "wildness." While some see the two as synonymous (Foreman, 1998), others (Snyder, 1990; Turner, 1996) see a "quality of mind" sense in wildness that is more powerful than a defense of wilderness places per se. It is worth noting that Thoreau, a writer who chose his words very carefully, elected to argue that it was "wildness" and not "wilderness" that was the preservation of the world.

For Thoreau, then, direct experiences in Nature become educative. They, as Rothenberg illustrates, teach us "how to think." We can see, then, that, in the Romantic current, "experience" becomes an idea that is coupled with wilderness and with direct contact and individual embodiment with nature. Added to this is both an epistemological and a normative claim. First, knowledge is attained through these experiences and, second, such knowledge becomes the seeds of both individual transformation and societal reform. As Thoreau wrote in arguably the most influential text in American environmental thought, *Walking*:

> I had prepared myself to speak a word now for *Nature*—for the absolute freedom and wildness, as contrasted with a freedom and culture simply civil—to regard man as an inhabitant, or a part and parcel of nature—rather than a member of society. I wish to make an extreme statement, if so I may make an emphatic one, for there are enough champions of civilization— the minister and the school committee—and every one of you will take care of that.
>
> *quoted in Dean, 2007, p. 82*

Notice here that Thoreau places the "school committee" as a "champion of civilization" and speaks of Nature and "absolute freedom and wildness" as set apart from it. If schooling equals civilization and, like Rousseau, civilization is, to a large degree, the cause of the current ills of the world, then it follows that a move toward education-in-Nature is the reform that is needed. To Thoreau and others in the Romantic Transcendental period of American environmental thought, wildness really was the preservation of the world. This theme would carry forward to become the central influence of the modern conservation movement (developed first in the United States and then "exported" around the world).[2]

One final note on the Romantic Transcendental movement in the United States: typical histories (like mine) tend to evoke the same figures—Emerson, Thoreau, and Muir for example. Roderick Nash's classic *Wilderness and the American Mind* perhaps best exemplifies this historical framework. But, as I mentioned in the previous chapter, we must remain attentive to whom we leave out of our story and, in this case, we must note the absence of women in this narrative. Carolyn Merchant (1989) and Kimberly Jarvis (2007) have noted that these histories leave out important early figures in the early wilderness conservation movement such as Mary King Sherman and, as a consequence, fail to understand the gendered nature of the our very concept of wilderness. To Jarvis (p. 150):

---

2 For criticisms of "environmental imperialism" see Guha (1998), "Radical American Environmentalism and 'Wilderness' Preservation: A Third World Critique," Parajuli (2001), "Do Four Trees Make a Jungle?", and Rothenberg & Ulvaeus (2001), *The World and the Wild*.

the politics of wilderness between 1870 and 1930 were in many ways linked to gender politics. Although the idea of wilderness was attractive to both men and women, wilderness was often referred to in masculine terms. Rugged and dangerous, wilderness experiences required physical strength and endurance, which would counterbalance the effects of the more effeminate modern urban life that many Americans believed threatened American masculinity . . . Saving wilderness, then, was also saving American manhood and, by extension, the nation.

Women were certainly marginalized from the dominant notions of "rugged individualism" espoused in the early wilderness conservation movement, but that did not mean they were not present or influential in the early formation of our conservation ethic. Jarvis notes that many American women such as Sherman served as "the foot soldiers" of the movement by writing letters, donating money, and advocating for increased preservation and protection of America's wild places. There is certainly much more work that can be done here not just with revealing the key roles women played but other subaltern voices including Native Americans, African-Americans, and other immigrant groups in the United States as well as a broader history of international voices on our notions of wilderness and nature.

Legacies of Romanticism

The educational legacy of Romanticism runs deep in Western intellectual history. As Berlin notes, "the great achievement of romanticism . . . was that, unlike most other great movements in human history, it succeeded in transforming certain of our values to a very profound degree" (1999, p. 139). For our purposes here, it is worth briefly touching upon one aspect of the romantic legacy—existentialism—while noting other resonant themes that strongly influence experiential education before carrying forth to criticisms of this legacy. Berlin notes that existentialism is the "truest heir of romanticism" (p. 139) and, to no surprise, elements of it are evoked with some frequency in curricular theorizing in experiential education. Many students of education are familiar with A. S. Neill's Summerhill School in England as a, perhaps extreme, example of existential approaches to schooling. Neill, like Rousseau, believed strongly in organizing the curriculum around student ownership of learning. Summerhill, founded in 1921, is often referred to as one of the original "free schools" and allows students an unusual degree of freedom in managing their own affairs. On the current school website (2010), Neill is quoted as saying: "the function of a child is to live his own life—not the life that his anxious parents think he should live, not a life according to the purpose of an educator who thinks he knows best" (retrieved November 10, 2010 from http://www.summerhillschool.co.uk/pages/asneill.html). Existentialism's maxim that "existence precedes essence" connects to the experiential education project in valuing inductive learning over objectified and universal truths. With this approach, a child needs to practice out her existence. She needs to test, to fail, even sometimes to suffer in order to truly learn. Maxine Greene (1988), perhaps our best voice on existential perspectives in education today, noted (p. 22):

> Fundamentally, perhaps, I am conscious of the tragic dimension in every human life. Tragedy, however, discloses and challenges; often, it provides images of men and women on the verge. We may have reached a moment in our history when teaching and learning, if they are to happen meaning- fully, must happen on the verge. Confronting a void, confronting nothing- ness, we may be able to empower the young to create and re-create a common world—and, in cherishing it, in renewing it, discover what it signifies to be free.

Freedom, for existentialists, must entail a "lived experience." It is not understood through abstraction, book learning, or logic. It is lived. In terms of schooling, then, the curriculum must be organized in such a way as to maximize the under- standing that comes through living, through experience. This is why A.S. Neill organized Summerhill the way he did. It is why existentialist schools today provide broad latitude for individual choice and collective, democratic decision- making. And, this stance has its roots in the romantic legacy we have been exploring. As Greene notes: "there are echoes of an old romanticism in this attitude, of old rebellions against mechanisms, schedules, clocks, crowds" (1988, p. 20). Experiential curricula, more often than not, set themselves up against "traditional" education. This dichotimzation mirrors Whitman's poem of the Learn'd Astronomer and Thoreau's admonition of civilization and the school board. Experiential learning is "outside"—literally and figuratively— the mainstream. It is meant as a conscious form of rebellion in a sense. It is a rebellion against tradition, against Enlightenment notions of progress, intelli- gence, and human worth. Whether it is in place-based education, service learning, adventure education, or other myriad experiential projects, there exists an element of insurgency, of "wildness" in the Thoreauian sense, against the status quo of education, and existentialism continues this legacy in education today.

The legacy of Romanticism continues beyond existentialism to several key themes that play out in myriad experiential education projects today. The notion of the importance of "direct, unmediated experience" is a warp-thread that runs through virtually all modern experiential projects. Itin (1999), for example, defines experiential learning as "the change in an individual that results from reflection on a *direct experience* and results in new abstractions and applications" (p. 93, emphasis added). The Romantic legacy places high value on the individual learner engaging with unmediated (and therefore powerful) experience. This gets picked up and employed within modern-day experiential projects as evidenced below in a rather classic sentiment from the field:

> Some feel about experiential education the way Hemingway felt about making love: Don't talk about it, you'll only ruin the experience. We know it's good because it feels good, and as G. E. Moore, the philosopher said: good is good, and that's the end of the matter. It can only be defined in terms of itself, it has intrinsic worth so there is no other standard to judge it by, it requires no further justification. The values are self-evident. Let the mountains speak for themselves!
>
> *Nold, cited in Warren et al., 1995, p. 113*

Letting the "mountains speak for themselves" implies that the most powerful learning comes from a sense that experience is, truly, the best teacher. Such value statements reflect Thoreau's admonition for "Contact! Contact!" as well as romantic and existential belief in the power of direct experience to "place in students' hands the exhilarating power to follow trails of interest, to make connections, to reformulate ideas, and to reach unique conclusions" (Brooks & Brooks, 1999, p. 22).

The belief in the innate goodness of the child and the power of individual choice is also present in many (if not all) experiential curricula. The resurgent movement for and interest in unstructured play, as evidenced by the popularity of Richard Louv's *Last Child in the Woods* and the "No Child Left Inside" movement, attest to the romantic and existential influence of freedom-in-Nature. Too much structure, too much discipline, in this worldview, "disciplines" experience and threatens its transformative potential. Dorothy Lee (1986) evokes this sense when she speaks of the power of labels and their ability to stifle experience for a child (p. 42):

> Are we paying a heavy price for literacy? Are we giving up our heritage of wonder, of curiosity, of questing, of plunging into chaos and creating life out of it? Are we giving up our sense of mystery, the excitement of being lost in ambiguity and building a world out of it? Have we given up this heritage for the sake of literacy, which gives us a label instead of experience?

Lee's questioning of something as taken for granted as literacy speaks to the counter-cultural elements woven into the romantic sensibility. Labels (like "literacy") come from society, while experience emerges from the unmediated contact between the individual and her environment. To Lee, and many others within this current, the central aim of education ought to be to provide opportunities to learn from experience before learning from labels. This simple notion of "experience before label" captures a key current within our river. Herein lies the potential for a transformative function of education. Like elements of existentialism, that potential is ultimately a liberating potential. It is through the power of experience that we become free. As we shall see, however, this freedom can be framed in very different ways. Here, in the romantic current, this freedom is couched with an individualistic slant.

One final legacy of Romanticism worth noting here is the notion of the "strange lands" journey. From Thoreau and John Muir and even Aldo Leopold there is a sense that the sublime can be achieved only through immersive journey (what Leopold famously described as necessitating a two-week pack into the wilderness). Richard Kraft (1995) describes this as a "strange lands" experience while connecting wilderness experiences with cross-cultural ones (p. 158):

> As we look back at Walsh and Golin's explanation of the Outward Bound process, it becomes evident that the international setting has many of the same characteristics . . . I am convinced that properly designed international experiences can be and are among the most powerful "life changing" experiences that we as learners can have. While the wilderness environment takes away many of the traditional environmental cues for city dwellers and suburbanites, "strange lands" change not only the environmental setting but take away most of the linguistic, cultural, religious, political, and other cues with which we have grown accustomed.

Here we see how the "strange lands" experience (whether in nature/wilderness or in another culture) has transformative potential for the student and how it requires a journey. One cannot have such an experience in the comfort of everyday experience. It must involve dislocation. We can see such an emphasis in experiential education through the notions of the "expedition," through service learning trips to New Orleans ninth ward (a section of the city hit particularly hard by flooding in the aftermath of Hurricane Katrina), through environmental education centers located not in the middle of cities but rather out in the woods, or in international study. In each, a direct unmediated, "strange lands" experience is possible only through an immersive journey.

Limitations of the Romantic Current in Experiential Education

Criticisms of Romantic orientations within experiential education are relatively recent (Hirsch, 1996; Fenwick, 2001; Fox, 2008; Roberts, 2008; Seaman, 2008) but growing area of scholarship in the field. Outside the field of experiential education, criticisms of the romantic legacy have a longer and more pronounced history. For our purposes here, we will summarize the central arguments under four broad areas: critique of the autonomous learner, of unmediated and direct experience, of innocent notions of "wilderness" and "nature," and the concept of the sublime as a catalyst for transformative learning.

The Autonomous Learner

First, and as indicated in the title to this chapter, experience within this current becomes a particularly individual phenomenon. This is not to say that the social milieu around the individual learner is not accounted for. Particularly within some forms of existentialism, there exists an element of social consciousness around the learning process. Maxine Greene and Simone de Beauvoir are examples of theorists who very consciously bring existentialism out from a retreat "into themselves." Nonetheless, implicit in the Romantic legacy is the idea of the unique and autonomous individual. As Hay (2002) notes, for example, the Romantic tradition represents the "triumph of extreme individualism" (p. 7). Hess (2010) argues that most nature writers of the Romantic tradition construct a solitary and individual subject when they "exemplify a wider pattern in environmental writing, the celebration of heightened moments in which the solitary self experiences 'nature' apart from other human beings, work, and other practical activity" (p. 8). He goes on to say that:

> The tendency to isolate the self from social and economic relationship is in this way present not only in wilderness writing, but in the rich tradition of environmental writing about more ordinary environments as well. Thoreau writes about his cabin at Walden pond in a way that turns it into a kind of imaginative wilderness solitude, though he can see the railroad from his cabin a few hundred yards away along the shore of the pond and uses its tracks for his almost daily walks into town. Thoreau also neglects to mention his regular dinners with his family, the Emersons, and other friends; his periodic raids on his mother's cookie jar (literally); or the other social and economic networks which sustained him in his supposed self-sufficiency.

This emphasis on individual autonomy that has been taken up within experiential education has significant problems. Hay (2002) describes Emerson's sense of experience in Nature: "His romanticism thus proclaims a supreme and sovereign individual—one that is almost god-like—and the function of nature is to serve as the medium for the individual's attainment of a state of high exaltation of the spirit" (p. 8). Bell (1993) notes that "many characterizations of experiential education seem pre-occupied with individual change and lack 'clear sociological analysis'" (quoted in Seaman, 2008, p. 9). And Michelson (1996) argues that "underneath the avowal that community is indispensable is a longing for a unitary, authentic self untouched by the demands of human mutuality" (p. 140). The construction of the radically autonomous individual within the Romantic current has the tendency to gloss over the social construction of experience, and, as a result, can fail to incorporate issues of power, particularly around issues of identity (e.g., race, class, gender, sexual orientation). Service learning projects, international study experiences, even experiential classroom projects that are framed as individual experiences may be "transcendent" in some respects but may also lift such experiences out of their important social and political contexts. Furthermore, the emphasis on "freedom" and "choice" makes this construction of experience vulnerable to cooptation by larger market forces. If individual choice is the highest educational good, how do we distinguish between that and the dominant values of consumerism that take virtually the identical stance? This is an issue we will explore in more depth in Chapter 6.

"Direct" Experience

A second critique emerges out of the notion of "raw and unmediated" experience within this variation. "Direct experience" in this variation is seen as not only possible but preferable as a transcendent expression of being fully human. But is experience quite so raw and unmediated? Do the mountains really "speak for themselves"? Holman et al. (1997) argue that, within this paradigm, experience "is seen as pure, unproblematic, fully accessible by conscious thought, possessing a presymbolic quality which exists prior to meaning attached to it. The text of experience will always be able to be read. Its meaning will always be apparent and decipherable" (p. 138). By contrast, for pragmatists, as we will see in the next chapter, lived experience is always seen as relational and transactional. That is, there is no point in discussing or attempting to retrieve or identify the "authentic" or transcendent individual experience as it is located not solely within the consciousness of the experiencing subject but rather in the interplay between the subject and her surroundings. As Dewey noted:

> The pragmatist starts from a much more commonplace notion of experi-
> ence, that of the plain man who never dreams that to experience a thing is
> first to destroy the thing and then to substitute a mental state for it. More
> particularly, the pragmatist has insisted that experience is a matter of
> functions and habits, of active adjustments and re-adjustments, of coordi-
> nations and activities, rather than states of consciousness.
>
> *quoted in Kadlec, 2007, p. 21*

Post-structuralist theorists have noted that experience is not as "raw" as we presume but rather very mediated by social and discursive conditions. Claudia Ruitenberg (2005), in her analysis of place-based education, argues that the romantic constructions of experiences-in-place are seemingly ignorant of the power of mediated lives. She notes (p. 214):

> Derrida contends that there is no such thing as direct, unmediated
> experience. No experience is fully present to the consciousness of the
> experiencing subject; each experience leaves traces in that warehouse of

remnants called the Unconscious and is itself shaped by the conscious and unconscious discursive categories that have previously left their marks on the body and the mind of the experiencing subject.

What do we assume when we take it for granted that experience is direct and unmediated? This construction of experience, born from the Romantic legacy, represents a significant limitation in several visible, contemporary curriculum projects in experiential education including service learning, place-based education, and environmental education.

Back to Nature

As we explored earlier, there is a back-to-nature thread that runs through the Romantic temperament. From Rousseau to Whitman and Thoreau, learning happens best, it seems, in Nature and Wilderness. But, like experience, these concepts are not quite as self-evident as they seem. Callicott (1998) and Cronon (1996) are perhaps most well-known in their critique of the "received" wilderness ideal. To both, "wilderness" is, in fact, a social construction that does not exist outside of human meaning-making. Callicott cites examples from history whereby "wilderness" was declared only after Native Americans were removed from the land, making it "empty" and thus worthy of wilderness designation. He writes of European colonization of the Americas: "[t]he European immigrants in fact found a man-made landscape, but they thought it was a wilderness because it didn't look like the man-made landscape that they had left behind" (1998, p. 353). Cronon extends this by examining the effects of dichotomizing civilization and wilderness. "This, then, is the central paradox: wilderness embodies a dualistic vision in which the human is entirely outside the natural. If we allow ourselves to believe that nature, to be true, must also be wild, then our very presence in nature represents its fall" (1996, p. 484). In response to such criticisms, several wilderness proponents have responded that the deconstruction of the wilderness ideal has gone too far (Foreman, 1998; Turner, 1996), arguing that dismissing direct experience with "wilderness" leaves us incapable of defending critical ecological areas while, at the same time, constructing a disturbingly anthropocentric environmental ethic.

Beyond the more particular notion of "wilderness," "Nature" as a larger philosophical construct has also been under sustained interrogation as a taken-for-granted term in the literature (Bonnett, 2004). Hess (2010) summarizes many of the problems associated with a Romantic construction of experience-in-Nature (p. 4):

[T]here are few positive imaginative and ecological models to encourage deep commitment to the unspectacular, developed, aesthetically ordinary environments where most of us live and work. If students take an environmental literature class in Richmond, Indiana, or most other parts of the country, they are likely to be encouraged to imagine, desire, and value a landscape far away—a landscape they can hope to visit, perhaps, but where very few will ever live. The idea of nature in such writing is likely to lead them to a form of imaginative and spiritual tourism, and hence to the opposite of commitment to place. It will also likely teach them to construct their identity as autonomous individuals, defined in relationship to "nature" but apart from human social, cultural, and economic relationships, and hence through a form of physical and imaginative escape.

While the wilderness ideal was perhaps an easier target for criticism, "Nature" has proved a much more contested construct, and the response to the postmodern turn in environmental philosophy has been vigorous (Bonnet, 2004; Soulé et al., 1995). Regardless of one's philosophical stance on "wilderness" or "Nature," it is clear that, similar to "experience," one cannot merely accept the taken-for-granted notions of such terms and employ them without critical reflection. It is curious that the field of experiential education (with the exception of a small subsection within environmental education[3]) has yet to significantly engage with this on-going debate.

The Sublime

One final limitation of the Romantic construction of educative experience involves the notion of the sublime. The Romantic sense of the sublime comes from the Latin *sublimis* (to look up from). It involves a sense of magnitude, greatness, and other-worldliness. Nash argues that "the concept of sublimity gained widespread usage in the eighteenth century. As an aesthetic category the sublime dispelled the notion that beauty in nature was seen only in the comfortable, fruitful, and well-ordered. Vast, chaotic scenery could also please" (1982, p. 45). Beyond the well-kept English garden, the wild places far removed from the cultural comforts of urban and even rural life held the key to transcendence and a closer association to God. Because these new sublime places were set apart from civilization and the city, it often took a journey (either real or metaphoric) to access these feelings. One literally had to leave the more debased material realm and ascend to a higher plane. This sense led Muir to claim that the solitude of the wilderness "is a sublime mistress, but an intolerable wife" (quoted in Nash, 1982, p. 126). And here we see the problem. Wilderness and the sublime feelings it evokes are always temporary—like a visit to a mistress that, while potentially pleasurable, entails the hard crash back down to the realities of domesticity and the everyday.[4] We may have powerful, transformative, and direct

---

3 See Bonnett (2004), Bowers (2003), and Orr (2002) for more on this line of thinking.

experiences in distant, sublime, and wild places, but, upon return and re-entry into "civilization" and our more "debased" local spaces and places, do the feelings linger?

This reminds us of the classic children's tale by Maurice Sendak, *Where the Wild Things Are*. In it, Max must leave his room and go on a journey "in and out of weeks and almost over a year to where the wild things are." While he has quite an experience there (including a wild rumpus), Max eventually longs for home and sails back "in and out of weeks" to his room where he finds his supper "and it was still hot." Max's journey is emblematic of a certain framework within Romantic constructions of experiential education. The educational journey often involves a trip to another place (not the classroom) and that place is often the location of a more powerful, sublime, and thus transcendent experience. As a consequence of this emphasis on raw, unmediated experience, the experience itself takes on a special and sublime quality. Owing to the heightened awareness of sensorial experience, lived experience becomes something "special" as opposed to something "everyday." Drawing from the Romantic tradition, truly trans-formative experience is that which takes us away from the everyday and the typical. Thus the most powerful lived experiences happen somewhere else, not "here." It requires Kraft's "strange lands experience." While pragmatist orienta-tions to experience, which we will explore in the next chapter, wish to use the concept to collapse the false dichotomy between the "real world" and the school world, experience within the Romantic current seems to capitalize on the difference between the two in order to signal the significance and novelty of the experience outside the four-walled classroom.

Somehow, the lived experiences of the Romantic current are "special" experi-ences. And yet, what happens upon re-entry? Does the very construction of experience as "Other" preclude its transference back to the "real world"? This is seemingly an unresolvable contradiction written into Romantic constructions of experience and, as a result, it ought to come as no surprise that "transfer" from such experiences to the everyday remains a problematic outcome for experiential educators. Too often, students on such sublime experiences struggle upon return to the "real world." It is not quite as easy as Max's return to his room in *Where the Wild Things Are* where he finds his bowl of soup "still hot." With "strange lands" experiences, the more we seem to amplify the differences, the more we make it difficult for learners to reconcile those differences upon return. And yet, it is that very difference that makes the experience powerful in the first place. Moving forward, working through these possibilities and limitations of the Romantic legacy in experiential education will be crucial.

---

4 I am well aware of the gendered constructions used by Muir here. It is important to recognize that this was the zeitgeist of the era under exploration. See Merchant (1989) and Jarvis (2007) for more on this issue.

Conclusion

With these limitations are we then to discard Romanticism and its construction of experiential education? No. We can no more discard it than we can remove a particular current in a river by attempting to block its path with a paddle or our hand. The water simply and effortlessly moves around the obstruction. But we can be aware of both the possibilities and the limitations of Romantic constructions of experience. It is possible to still enjoy the out-of-the-classroom approaches (they are usually fun after all and quite educative) with eyes wide open. In 2009, I taught a course entitled "Pedagogies of Place" where, for part of the semester, we purposefully engaged with place-based learning activities by using the local river that runs through town. Three months after the course, as part of a research grant, I asked students to reflect on what, if anything, still resonated from the course. One student remarked:

> In reflecting back on the Pedagogies of Place class, what stands out most to me are the "field trips" and the opportunities we had to be outside and meet people who were in direct relationship with the places and concepts we were studying. When I think about the highlights of this class my mind is immediately flooded with images of the Farris [*sic*] family farm, particularly of sitting around the fire together that evening and telling stories, having both faculty, alumni, students and community members reflecting and sharing in a way that seems impossible to find in a classroom. Under the stars and camped out cross-legged in a circle, it seemed we were experiencing something somehow especially "real" and meaningful, an experience that, if nothing else, would stay with me and mark a powerful moment in the course as well as my semester and perhaps all of my time at Earlham.
>
> Thinking about this as I write I am reminded of our class conversations of Thoreau and other romantics and our discussions of the tendencies and challenges of "romanticizing" nature and the natural world. While perhaps I am doing this now, there is something undeniably striking about the direct experience of being in and learning from the outdoors. Interestingly, these experiences were not limited to and hardly included moments in the "Great Outdoors" as an expansive wilderness, but rather simply anything outside of the four walls of the Earlham classroom and "in" and among the greater space, place and community we were exploring. While the theory and readings assigned in class certainly deepened and gave meaning to the other activities, it is the moments outside and with other people that most stand out to me. It seems that with my hands wet and my clothes dirty, the ideas and concepts we were studying began to take shape and come to life.

Here, Jane[5] exemplifies many of the themes we have been discussing in this chapter. She speaks of the power of "direct experience" and the realness of being "under the stars" and she sets this against her everyday experiences at college. But she does not stop there. She continues in the second paragraph to critically reflect on that particular view of education and nature and reinscribes the enterprise as "anything outside the four walls" and "in and among the greater space, place, and community." This does not "fix" some of the problems we have explored in this particular current but, at the very least, she is aware of the limitations. The reason this is one of the most powerful currents in experiential education is that, quite simply, it works. The Romantic legacy of bringing emotion, sentiment, and personal experience back into balance with reason has had a profound influence on countless students and educators. It is not to be dismissed lightly. But, in its very strength, in the seductive pull of its current, we must be cautious not to be swept away.

5   The student's name has been changed.

4

EXPERIENCE AND THE SOCIAL

The Pragmatist Current

Shared experience . . . is the greatest of human goods.

John Dewey

Introduction

When Charles Sanders Peirce declared, in his *Collected Papers*, that "experience is our only teacher" (quoted in Houser & Klousel, 1992, p. xxxiv), he punctuated a particular period in philosophy now known as American Pragmatism. And it is this philosophical tradition that forms the intellectual energy for our next current in experiential education: the social current. It is certainly true that, for Romantics such as Rousseau, Thoreau, and Emerson, experience, too, was the only teacher. So what sets this particular current apart? In order to answer this, we'll need to wade into some of the central tenets of pragmatic thought, what Richard Bernstein labeled as the "pragmatist ethos" (1992). This will allow us to see the ways in which experience, as constructed in pragmatist theory, can be framed as decidedly *social* and *transactional* in orientation. From here, we'll dive down deep into the writings and work of John Dewey—unquestionably the most significant figure in this current if not in the field of experiential education as a whole. Our trajectory will be somewhat unconventional. Rather than begin with *Experience and Education*, Dewey's 1938 classic that is perhaps his most cited and influential work in relation to education, we'll begin with another, less widely read text, *Art as Experience*, in an effort to weave the pragmatist ethos into an understanding of Dewey's particular construction of experience. Finally, we'll surface and take a look at how this social construction of experience impacts contemporary curriculum projects in experiential education, noting, as we did with the Romantic current, the possibilities and limitations of this particular current of experience.

The Pragmatist Ethos

Typically, we learn about John Dewey in education through the philosophy of "educational progressivism." Most students taking courses in education, for example, don't hear much about Dewey's philosophical association with pragmatism. On the other hand, students in philosophy classes rarely hear about Dewey's educational projects and focus much more on his contributions to pragmatic thought. This can get confusing. Was Dewey a progressivist or a pragmatist? The answer is "yes," he was both. To further muddy the water, progressivism is not just an educational philosophy per se. It can also be referred to as a social and political movement that emerged around the same time as pragmatism (the late nineteenth century through to the early twentieth century). In an attempt to clear up terms, we might think of pragmatism as a particular philosophical school of thought characterized through the early work of Charles Sanders Peirce and William James in the 1870s and furthered by figures such as John Dewey and George Herbert Mead up through the middle part of the twentieth century. Progressivism (the socio-political movement) began at roughly the same time and emerged as a set of ideals around making society more just and more equitable—especially given the urban upheavals brought about by industrialization and immigration. *Educational* progressivism developed as a specific application of progressive ideals drawing heavily from the work of John Dewey in how he translated a pragmatic philosophy to the practical enterprise of schooling. It quickly took on a life of its own through the work of practitioners such as Francis Parker, Jane Addams, and William Wirt in his work with the schools in Gary, Indiana. Educational progressivism, and Dewey's role in its construction, have been well documented in the literature on the origins of experiential education. What has been less explored, and what will be important for our understanding here, is the influence of pragmatism on the notion of experience and how, through its distinctive epistemological claims, it sets up a distinctive shift from the Romantic current in our thinking about the role of experience in education.

Yet, as with our previous exploration of Romanticism, it is dangerous to assume some cohesive intellectual stance amongst the variety of individuals who have been variously labeled as pragmatists. There is no one "pragmatism" in the sense that these theorists all agreed on some coherent platform. In fact, Peirce and James, for example, did not agree on much, leading Peirce to attempt, rather humorously at one point, to call his own thought "pragmaticism" as a way of distinguishing between his and James's ideas. Martin Jay described them as a "family of thinkers" (2005, p. 269) and was quick to note that the concept should also include the prominent African-American intellectuals W. E. B. Du Bois and Alain Locke in addition to Europeans such as Theodore Flournoy and Giovanni Papini. Yet, while there is no one, true "pragmatism," we *can* safely discuss a few general philosophical stances that are understood to be well within the territory that most, if not all, pragmatists cover.

A basic and defining characteristic of pragmatism is its keen interest on examining things based upon practical consequences. This is where the more popularized sense of the term "pragmatic" comes from. To be pragmatic is to be practical. In other words, one chooses the right course of action on the basis of the likelihood of success or with an awareness of the consequences of one's actions. In many ways, this stance draws from the scientific method. Pragmatists such as Mead and Dewey were immensely influenced by Darwinian science and the process of the scientific method to discern the right courses of action. Rather than relying on a form of abstracted reason, the experimental nature of science where hypotheses were introduced, tested, reformulated, and tested again functioned as the ideal metaphor for a pragmatic epistemology. How do we know? We formulate hypotheses based upon what we think might happen, then we test them out, reflect on the consequences of those actions, and then reformulate again. Of course, central to this stance is a robust notion of experience. As historian James Kloppenberg relates, "[pragmatists believed that] meaning must be interpreted on the basis of lived experience and informed with an understanding of the reflected experience of life" (quoted in Jay, 2005, p. 271).

Experience, to pragmatists, is the ultimate teacher because it allows for a more "enlightened" sense of empiricism. Rather than seeing empiricism as nothing more than individual sense data or some sort of fetish of the minute and measurable, pragmatists viewed empiricism, in the form of experience, as a way to examine meaning and value broadly and rigorously. William James (1907) provides a nice analogy of a classroom that drives this point home (pp. 8–9):

> [A young graduate] began by saying that he had always taken for granted that when you entered a philosophic classroom you had to open relations with a universe entirely distinct from the one you left behind you in the street. The two were supposed, he said, to have so little to do with each other, that you could not possibly occupy your mind with them at the same time. The world of concrete personal experiences to which the street belongs is multitudinous beyond imagination, tangled, muddy, painful and perplexed. The world to which your philosophy-professor introduces you is simple, clean and noble. The contradictions of real life are absent from it. . . . In point of fact it is far less an account of this actual world than a clear addition built upon it . . . It is no explanation of our concrete universe.

By linking thinking with a consideration of practical consequences, pragmatists opened the door to a more robust construction of experience that placed it at the center of the philosophical enterprise. No longer was abstract theorizing the only "account of this actual world" as James points out. It is only by linking personal experience (practice) to theory that we have a true account of the world.

This line of thinking was a direct challenge to the Cartesian maxim "I think therefore I am" and to so-called analytic philosophers who believed that only a rigorous form of logic could peel back the veil and reveal truths about the world. To pragmatists, knowledge acquisition is inherently interactive. Dewey referred to this as the Copernican turn, recentering the epistemological universe away from the mind and toward a relational orientation. "The old center was the mind . . . [t]he new center is indefinite interactions" (1927/1954, p. 232). To pragmatists, thinking cannot be removed from the world in which we live. It would be better to say that we think/act. It is the interaction between the two, and how the two revise each other, that brings about new awareness and learning. This is how experience, in pragmatist thought changes from a noun to a *verb*. Experience is action. Or, more to the point, it is trans-action.

Connected to this transactional epistemology is the notion of the social nature of self or "transactional constructivism" (Biesta & Burbules, 2003, p. 11). Here, we begin to see the contrast between romantic and pragmatic constructions of experience come into focus. To pragmatists, experience is not an individual mental state in the sense that we explored it within the Romantic current. This is because individual experience, in pragmatist thought, is realized only in transaction with others. This can most clearly be seen in George Mead's discussion of the "gesture." A gesture, to Mead, is the "first overt phase in a social act" (Biesta & Burbules, 22003, p. 4). Mead uses an example of a dog-fight to explain the concept further. The act of growling from one animal provides the stimulus for the other animal. This action-stimulus creates a relationship between the two. The response of the second dog to the growl of the first in turn stimulates the first to change his position or attitude. "What we have here is a conversation of gestures" (Mead, 1934, p. 43). However, Mead makes the important distinction that the conversations of gestures represented in a dog-fight are not, yet, significant. What makes a gesture significant is reflective consciousness. Individuals do not stimulate and respond sequentially as the previous dog-fighting example might indicate. Rather, individuals *anticipate* and adjust their attitude toward the other—they interpret what the other's action might lead to. To Mead then, experience is a meaning-guided activity and, most importantly, the meanings of gestures do not have their origin within the individual, nor do they have some objectively discernable meaning. Rather, the meaning is inter-subjective: it is located in-between individuals.

Thus far we have two key tenets of a pragmatist ethos—the importance of practical consequences and the interactive and social sense of experience. A third element brings in the importance of context. In order to consider practical consequences interactively, one must be situated *somewhere*. Problem-solving, to pragmatists, is inherently contextual—the way one might conceive of the effects in one environment might not be the same as another. And, the interactions one has in one place may not be the same as another. This contextualized form of reason leads to a third element of a pragmatic ethos: anti-foundationalism. Because right courses of action are generated from experimentation in unique times and places, universal rules or foundations that can be generally applied to all situations simply do not work. Each unique problem must be addressed within an inter-active, experimental context. We cannot apply universal laws to problems because truth claims will necessarily be different in different contexts and, importantly, at different times.

This, in turn, leads to a final characteristic of the pragmatist ethos: "fallibilism." Because there is no fixed truth, it is likely that, when attempting to discern best courses of action, we can be wrong. Such errors are part of learning. As Bernstein (1992) relates, "for the pragmatists, contingency and chance are not merely signs of human ignorance, they are ineradicable and pervasive features of the universe" (p. 329). Thus, we can know only partially and what we know is in constant revision. In essence, this is a call for "trial and error" learning. We learn as much when we are wrong about something as when we are right. This emphasis on the contingent and fallible nature of knowledge leaves pragmatism in the somewhat awkward position of considering that pragmatism, too, is fallible. If we cannot readily arbitrate between truth claims outside of their "usefulness" in specific situations, how do we know what is true? This has led some to claim that the very nature of pragmatist thought is paradoxical (Garrison & Neiman, 2003). Richard Rorty (1999) would pick up on this ironic and contingent epistemo-logical stance to bring pragmatism into the postmodern era.

These basic tenets of the pragmatic ethos should be recognizable to students and practitioners of experiential education—the importance of consequences, the interactive nature of knowledge, the social qualities of learning, the notion of context and contingency, and the significance of "trial and error." This should come as no surprise because, as we discussed earlier in this chapter, pragmatism serves as the intellectual root to educational progressivism. While educational progressivism is often set aside as an isolated methodological approach, its core philosophical positions connect it directly to pragmatism. And, the individual most recognized for linking these two domains is John Dewey. Dewey had the ability to bring a very robust philosophical stance to the practical problems of education and schooling and, in so doing, he practiced what he preached (linking theory to practice). While some feel that the lionization of Dewey is perhaps overdone, it is difficult to dismiss the sheer volume and significance of his work. Schubert et al. (2002) in their classic work, *Curriculum Books*, describe three historic schools of curriculum thought—intellectual traditionalists, social behavi-orists, and experientalists—and go on to claim that "although virtually all writers will be succeeded by other voices in their respective educational positions, Dewey is never superseded as spokesperson. Even today, he retains his posture as the single most significant voice of the experientialist perspective" (p. 13). It should be noted by way of introduction here that Jane Addams and Dewey's wife, Alice Chipman, were instrumental in "educating" Dewey on the importance of education—bringing him out of his ivory tower and into the practical problems of the world—an influence we will discuss later in this chapter.

Dewey's Notion of Experience

As the title of this book suggests, simply equating Dewey with a philosophy of "learning by doing" substantially misses the point. It is simplistic and, in some respects, even dangerous as we will explore in more detail in Chapter 7. But understanding Dewey's notion of experience represents a significant challenge for, in many respects, experience rests at the core of Dewey's epistemology as evidenced by the titles of some of his most influential works: *Experience and Nature* (1958), *Art as Experience* (1934), and *Experience and Education* (1938). To compound things further, for Dewey, experience moved beyond "mere" epistemology toward the potential to weave together many (if not all) aspects of life including moral, aesthetic, and spiritual dimensions. As Jay (2005) notes, while Dewey famously rejected the Hegelian quest for certainty, he "never lost its no less powerful quest for unity" (p. 288). Experience then, to the dismay of many of his critics, acted as that unifying force for Dewey. It held the ability to collapse the false dichotomy between spectatorial objectivism and subjective idealism. It placed epistemological endeavors "on the ground" through the focus on problem solving. And it rejected universalist tendencies in philosophy by constantly checking what is known against new information and contexts. And yet, despite this unifying ability, Dewey acknowledged that there were, in fact, various types of experience, making it foolhardy to reduce it to some sort of an essential nature. All this is to say that Dewey expected much from this seemingly simple term; indeed, he constructed his entire philosophical project around it.

So, how might we go about tackling this? Rather than begin with *Experience and Education* as most have done when trying to illustrate Dewey's thoughts on experience relating to education, we'll take a different line through the current. In paddling, to "ferry" means to essentially "slip" across the current in order to maneuver a boat from point A to point B. This is what we'll do here. Rather than tackle the current head-on, we'll ferry across by looking first at Dewey's notion of experience in *Art as Experience*. Doing this, I hope, will give a fuller sense of the variation *within* Dewey's notion of experience and, then, allow us to launch full force into the main current with an appreciation for how complex the pragmatist current is in our river. This variation within Dewey's notion of experience can be seen most clearly in two of Dewey's favorite subjects of exploration: art and science. By examining the role of experience in each of these areas, we'll see that, in fact, Dewey had a more nuanced and measured approach to experience that moved well beyond the "closet positivism" some of his critics maintain he held (Bowers, 2003; Diggins, 1994; Noddings, 2006).

Dewey and the Science of Experience

Dewey's respect for science as an epistemological endeavor is well documented. And, it is the area his critics find the most trouble with. Yet, it would be misguided to equate his attraction to the scientific method with the entirety of his notion of experience.[1] The most common citation of Dewey's construction of experience seems to be the one we see elucidated in texts like *Experience and Education* where he argues that, in times of turmoil, the educator is often pressured to appeal to "great truths" and fixed authority. And yet such approaches remain, to Dewey (1938, p. 86):

> so out of touch with all the conditions of modern life that I believe it is folly to seek salvation in this direction. The other alternative is systematic utilization of scientific method as the pattern and ideal of intelligent exploration and exploitation of the potentialities inherent in experience.

Many have read a passage such as this as a grand pronouncement from Dewey that the scientific (or experimental) method ought to function as the singular model for philosophy. A common summary description of Dewey's notion of experience equates it to the "hypothesis-testing" sequence seen in the scientific method. Experience, in this characterization, becomes both *action* in the form of doing in the world and *reflection* in the form of cumulative and contingent knowledge gained over time. In describing these aspects of his notion of experience, Dewey often used the scientist performing an experiment as a "real world" analogy to what he was trying to describe epistemologically. This had led many, particularly those on the Left, to dismiss Deweyian pragmatism as too beholden to science (and by association to modernism in general) to be of worth as a critical epistemology. Max Horkheimer and others in the German Frankfurt School of Critical Theory perhaps were most famously critical of Dewey in this regard. Horkheimer noted that "Dewey's positivist call for unity of sciences 'is the counterpart of modern industrialism, for which the factory is the prototype of human existence'" (Kadlec, 2007, p. 40). Richard Rorty once quipped "Dewey was at his best when he emphasized the similarities between philosophy and poetry, rather than when he emphasized those between philosophy and engineering" (quoted in Jay, 2005, p. 301). But was Dewey ignorant of the potential problems associated with equating experience with the experimental method? It seems difficult to fathom, whether you like Dewey or not, that such a careful and deliberate philosopher would make such a simple mistake. And yet, this central "flaw" has been the most oft-repeated in opposition to Deweyian pragmatism (often by those who otherwise support a general pragmatist episte-mology). But, as Biesta & Burbules (2003) note (p. 14, emphasis in text):

---

1 For more on this, see Allison Kadlec's (2007) discussion of critical theory and the critique of Dewey's scientism in *Dewey's Critical Pragmatism*, pp. 37–50. Also, Biesta & Burbules's (2003) discussion, "Was Dewey a Positivist?" in *Pragmatism and Educational Research*, pp. 14–18.

Dewey was very clear about the value and importance of what he commonly refers to as the "scientific method" because "its comparative maturity as a form of knowledge exemplifies so conspicuously the necessary place and function of experimentation." But he hastens to add that his appreciation for the *method* of the natural sciences "would be misinterpreted if it were taken to mean science is the only valid kind of knowledge."

Thus, to Biesta, Dewey's use of the scientific method as an *example* should not be equated with the entirety of his epistemological approach. In addition, it would be a mistake to assume that his use of the scientific method analogy meant Dewey was incapable of forming a critical sense in regards to modernism in general as Horkheimer, Habermas, and others have claimed. Indeed science, for Dewey, had the *potential* to be something different; something that collapsed the dualism between the lived experience of everyday life and the realm of reason that had been reinforced since Greek classical philosophy. As Kadlec (2007) notes (p. 44):

> Dewey's enthusiasm for the scientific method is not grounded in a positivistic desire for verification of objective facts or for prediction and control . . . Nor is Dewey's approach to science a vulgar or reductionist glorification of all things given, as Horkheimer or Gramsci would argue . . . For Dewey, science releases us from a fixed and static conception of the world, and presents in its place a dynamic world that is always in-the-making, always changing, ever open, and "so multiplex and far-reaching" that it cannot be contained in any cramped metaphysical vision that sets Reason over and above the world as it is experienced in everyday life.

This denigration of everyday experience, to Dewey, functioned to separate science from common sense and to further distance the Academy from on-the-ground problem solving. This is what Biesta & Burbules (2003) refer to as Dewey's notion of a "crisis of rationality" when reason and rationality become domains solely of the mind and the "hard facts of science and not with values, morals, feelings, emotions, and so on" (p. 17). Thus, science and the scientific method to Dewey were not a positivistic attempt to describe reality as "it really is." Rather, it was, following Darwin, one of the best *methods* at our disposal to account for a changing and dynamic world while grounding rationality in the lived experience of everyday life.

Dewey and the Art of Experience

While it is certainly clear that Dewey found much to like in the scientific method, it was not the sole analogy for his epistemology of experience. To gain a fuller understanding of the unifying potential of experience in Dewey's philosophy, one must also consider how he constructs experience within the realm of art. It is here that we see an entirely different type of experience—aesthetic experience. The philosophy of art and art appreciation has its own long and varied intellectual history that is beyond the scope of this analysis to cover in any detail. At a basic level, one of the key tensions in the philosophy of art centers on the art object and the appreciating subject. And in the middle of this debate lies the notion of experience. As Jay (2005) notes (p. 161):

> Should that experience imply disinterested contemplation of objects made by others or artistic self-fashioning in which one experiences the world as raw material for creative play? Should it exclude moral and cognitive considerations entirely or attempt to incorporate them in a totalized notion of human experience as its most robust and fulfilling?

Into this debate entered Dewey with his classic and, according to Jaus (1982) in *Aesthetic Experience*, pioneering achievement, *Art as Experience* (1934). Published toward the end of his career, *Art as Experience* represents a markedly different approach to experience from Dewey's more commonly cited "experimental method." Martin Jay (2005) notes that "it surprised those who had equated pragmatism with an instrumentalist and utilitarian scientism" (p. 162). Through his consideration of experience in art, Dewey attempted once again to seek out and destroy the dualisms that he thought represented the "wounds of modern life" (Jay, 2005, p. 162). In this case, the wounds entailed a construction of aesthetic experience in art that either argued for detached disinterestedness or, conversely, lapsed too easily into self-indulgent narcissism. To collapse this false dichotomy, Dewey focused on the notion of what it meant to have "an experience." And, in doing so, he sought to evoke *both* the notions of *Erlebnis* (unmediated and in-the-moment experience) and *Erfahrung* (reflective and cumulative experience) within what he described as "esthetic" experience:

> Experience in the degree in which it *is* experience is heightened vitality. Instead of being shut up within one's own private feelings and sensations, it signifies active and alert commerce with the world; at its height it signifies interpenetration of self and the world of objects and events . . . it is art in germ. Even in its rudimentary forms it contains the promise of that delightful perception which is esthetic experience.
>
> *Dewey, 1934, p. 18, emphasis in text*

Where this heightened sense of vitality does not exist, Dewey claims "we drift" (p. 41) and, while we may experience, we do not have *an* experience. This most often occurs, according to Dewey, when the experience is either too tightly bounded (providing no opportunity for a sense of ownership) or, conversely, too "loose" which can lead to "dissipation, incoherence, and aimless indulgence" (p. 42). This is classic Dewey. First, frame the problem as a perceived binary, in this case between a construction of the aesthetic experience in art as having to be either objective or subjective in orientation, and then proceed to collapse the dichotomy by claiming that it is, of course, both. To have *an* experience suggests an integration of both reflective thinking and in-the-moment doing and feeling (*Erlebnis and Erfahrung*). Notions of aesthetic experience that over-emphasize doing or a "lust for action" (p. 46) reduce art to "mere" everyday experience. Conversely, the crowding together of too many abstract impressions yields a "fleeting and sipping" sentimentality unconnected to "the realities of the world" (pp. 46–47). In placing these orientations in transaction with one another, Dewey attempts to unify what he perceives as an unnatural and artificial schism between the dispassionate art observer and the subjectively enclosed art-maker. And it is, once again, *experience* that provides the necessary continuity and interaction.

It is important, at this point, to note that Dewey's construction of experience in *Art as Experience* is much more than a mere curious side bar or tangent in an otherwise homogeneous body of work; it goes to the heart of the epistemological endeavor for Dewey. For example, in the chapter, "The Challenge to Philosophy," Dewey called the "pure experience" of art a "challenge to that systematic thought called philosophy" (1934, p. 285). Importantly, Dewey goes on in this chapter to describe how a philosopher, working through what an aesthetic experience entails, reveals his or her larger epistemological stance (p. 286):

> For this reason, while the theory of esthetics put forth by a philosopher is incidentally a test of the capacity of its author to have the experience that is the subject-matter of his analysis, it is also much more than that. It is a test of the capacity of the system he puts forth to grasp that nature of experience itself.

Thus, Dewey's notion of experience constructed here ought not to be viewed as an odd divergence to his more robust elucidation of the experimental method and the role of experience in the natural sciences. Rather, in Dewey's own words, it is how one works through "esthetic experience" that offers the truest test of the adequacy of one's philosophical project.

In this construction of experience, Dewey found some surprising allies. According to Martin Jay, none other than Theodor Adorno (a noted critical theorist) described him as the "unique and truly free John Dewey" and went on to claim that "no one expressed [the aesthetic experience] with greater candor than the pragmatist John Dewey" (2005, p. 166). Indeed, Jay goes on to note that Dewey's "aesthetic variant" of experience ought to be seen as a sort of "normative goal" (p. 166) rather than a claim about the world as it is. Here, just as with Dewey's treatment of science, we can see a clear critique of modernity and the role of culture in everyday life.

Zeal for doing, lust for action, leaves many a person, especially in this hurried and impatient human environment in which we live, with experience of an almost incredible paucity, all on the surface. No one experience has a chance to complete itself because something else is entered upon so speedily. What is called experience becomes so dispersed and miscellaneous as hardly to deserve the name.

Dewey, 1934, p. 46

As a normative goal and a constantly receding horizon, Dewey's framing of aesthetic experience has the ability to both critique and suggest new ways forward. This non-foundational and pragmatic orientation offers intriguing possibilities for a variety of projects. Richard Rorty recognized this in Dewey. So did, surprisingly, Theodor Adorno. Most surprising of all, however, is the fact that so many others have chosen to overlook this element of Dewey's philosophy, preferring instead the ease of labeling Dewey a relic of a modern era long gone by. While some will take issue with the claim that Dewey's notion of experience found in *Art as Experience* is a better or clearer representation of his epistemological stance than other works, it can nonetheless *at least* be claimed that equating Dewey with some simplistic form of scientific positivism is irresponsible at best.

Experience and Education

So, given the sub-currents that existed within Dewey's construction of experience, what, if anything, holds them together? Is it still tenable to make any claims about what Dewey meant by "experience"? Indeed, late in his life, Dewey almost gave up on the term owing to the ways it was misinterpreted and considered replacing it with arguably a much more awkward term, "culture." While it is certainly true that Dewey saw variations within his philosophy of experience, there also exist commonalities that allow for a more general discussion of experience and, of particular relevance to this project, *educative* experience. The notion of educative experience for Dewey allowed him to bring together a philosophical framework from which to build his pragmatic social agenda (particularly as it related to schooling). He believed that schooling was the cultural institution where experience could be perhaps most powerfully put into practice.

In *Experience and Education*, he uses education as a sort of testing ground for his overall philosophical project. And, in the process, he reminds his readers that his notion of experience was *neither* overly child-centered as some of his progressive allies assumed *nor* a call for some impoverished form of vocationalism as his conservative critics claimed. His first line in the book is telling: "Mankind likes to think in terms of extreme opposites. It is given to formulating its beliefs in terms of *Either-Ors*, between which it recognizes no intermediate possibilities" (1938, p. 17, emphasis in text). Written toward the end of his career, *Experience and Education* was, in many respects, his final attempt to explain what he meant by this term "experience." A scant ninety-one pages long, it focused almost entirely on his conceptualization of experience, using education as its pragmatic application:

> Thus we reach a technical definition of education: it is that reconstruction or reorganization of experience which adds to the meaning of experience, and which increases the ability to direct the course of subsequent experience. The increment of meaning corresponds to the increased perceptions of the connections and continuities of the activities in which we are engaged.
>
> *Dewey, 1938, pp. 76–77*

It is here that we see the key elements of an educative experience for Dewey. It must achieve a continuity in which the past and present interact to create the future, and the meaning of such interaction is directly correlative to the connections we make in the process. This "continuous reconstruction of experience" (Dewey, 1938, p. 80) defines what is essential in the educational endeavor and, as a pedagogical approach, is separate (and superior) to alternative notions of education, as preparation for future living, as recapitulation of the past, or as an unfolding toward definitive goals. These necessary conditions (continuity and interaction) set the stage for one of Dewey's central ethical claims: that learning does not happen merely for learning's sake. Rather, learning takes place with the understanding that knowledge has moral consequences that invite (and often demand) social action.

Yet experience and education are not equated in Dewey's philosophy. Not all experiences are educative. Some may simply be non-educative; others may be mis-educative. "Any experience is mis-educative that has the effect of arresting or distorting the growth of further experience" (Dewey, 1938, p. 25). We see here in Dewey the importance of individual agency as part of the educational endeavor. Individuals must be able to direct themselves (through habits formed by experience). But just as all experiences are not of equal worth, neither are all habits. To Dewey, individuals can lose their agency through the formation of certain habits brought on by mis-educative experiences.

> An experience may be immediately enjoyable yet promote the formation of a slack or careless attitude; this attitude then operates to modify the quality of subsequent experiences so to prevent a person from getting out of them what they have to give . . . Each experience may be lively, vivid, and "interesting," and yet their disconnectedness may artificially generate dispersive, disintegrated, centrifugal habits. The consequence of formation of such habits is inability to control future experiences.
>
> *Dewey, 1938, p. 28*

Here, Dewey connects his notion of mis-educative experience with the notion of aesthetic experience discussed earlier. In both, experiences that are "unbounded" become shallow, dispersive, and disintegrated. And again, we see the elements of criticality coming through his argument. To Dewey, mis-educative experiences do not simply affect an individual in the present, such experiences create habits that affect an individual's ability to experience a sense of agency in future endeavors. When we entertain students with "lively, vivid, and interesting" experiences that are "disconnected" (1938, p. 28), we run the risk of developing in them habits that negatively impact their ability to direct their own future. This disconnection functions as a form of isolation, something Dewey consistently fought against in all of its forms. Disconnected experiences are, in essence, isolated (and isolating) experiences. A better construction involved connecting the individual, and her experiences, to the larger community.

This connectedness fosters positive growth, both for the individual and for the larger social network of relations she is a part of. And this is one of the major reasons experience becomes social in the pragmatic current. At the core, most of Dewey's arguments related to schooling had to do with democracy and democratic living. Indeed, he penned a 378-page book with just that title, *Education and Democracy* (1916). To Dewey, democracy becomes "lived" through the interrelationships and interdependence of social relations bound together by experiences—both individual and collective. Such a formulation for Dewey functioned as a form of moral imperative. It is a must for a democratic community and, by extension, for individuals and societies to create the good life. Thus, it is in the connection of the individual to the democratic community that we see the true moral implications of mis-educative experience. To Dewey, it is not education but what *kind* of education that one must consider when thinking about the ethical consequences of schooling.

> The devotion of democracy to education is a familiar fact. The superficial explanation is that a government resting on popular suffrage cannot be successful unless those who elect and who obey their governors are educated . . . *But there is a deeper explanation. A democracy is more than a form of government; it is primarily a mode of associated living, of conjoint, communicated experience.*
>
> *Dewey, 1916, p. 87, emphasis added*

To Dewey then, shared, educative experience is both a foundation to a democratic society and a catalyst for future progress. It is the meaningful transaction between the individual and her community (through experience) that encourages and promotes a diversity of growth and development and creates "response-ability". This is how this current of experience is decidedly distinct from the Romantic current—it constructs a social, interactive sense of educative experience. And, it is this shared sense of experience that leads to *progress* and, consequently, a progressive agenda for education. "The obstacles which confront us are stimuli to variation, to novel response, and hence are occasions for progress" (Dewey, quoted in West, 1989, p. 88). In a world filled with political, economic, and social injustice, how will we seek to create the good life? To Dewey, it is a process achieved, in part, through the democratic potential of the school. It should be deeply troubling that the current political discourse on school reform appears to be claiming to achieve some of the same ends (equality, opportunity, liberty) through vastly different means—standardization, quantification, and high stakes accountability. It should be more troubling (as we will see later in Chapter 7) that the transformative potential of Dewey's philosophy is, as he feared, being misapplied by those who might be in the best position to offer meaningful alternatives to the current dominant narratives of school reform.

> There is no discipline in the world so severe as the discipline of experience subjected to the tests of intelligent development and direction. Hence the only ground I can see for even a temporary reaction against the standards, aims, and methods of the newer education *is the failure of educators who professedly adopt them to be faithful to them in practice . . . the greatest danger that attends its future is, I believe, the idea that it is an easy way to follow, so easy that its course may be improvised,*
>
> Dewey, 1938, p. 90, emphasis added

Beyond Dewey: Possibilities and Limitations

While Dewey is clearly the most prevalent voice on matters of experience and education in the pragmatist thought, there are other notable figures worth exploring, and in doing so we will see some of the possibilities and limitations within this current of experiential education. Dewey is of course only human and, while his ideas have had far-reaching effects, they have not been without significant criticism. As we remain attentive to the stories we tell and the stories we leave out in this account of experience, it is crucial to realize the limitations of constructing this current as beginning and ending with John Dewey. Increasingly we are learning more about the role played by women in the early American pragmatist movement. Jane Addams (1860–1935), for example, is a key early contributor to our understanding of the intersections between experiential education, service learning, and social justice. Founder of Hull House and the recipient of the Nobel Peace Prize (something her more "famous" male pragmatist counterparts could certainly not claim), Addams was the pragmatist most noted for her ability to model the connections between theory and practice. It should come as no surprise that Addams was a good friend of John Dewey, often lecturing in his classes at the University of Chicago. She also corresponded frequently with other noted pragmatist thinkers including W. E. B. Dubois and William James. Addams distrusted abstract theorizing separated from everyday experience and sought to create an educational environment where the "school world" and the "real world" blended seamlessly with one another. Hull House was a wonderful illustration of this philosophy in practice. Founded in 1889, Hull House was a full-service social and educational center for the working poor and immigrant families of Chicago. Classes were offered, free concerts were held, social services were provided, and the house even became a center for legislative advocacy for the living conditions of the working poor. Educative experience, to Addams, was by definition social. It linked individuals to each other and to their communities. It connected learning to the essential values of democracy and social justice. And, it collapsed the false divide between the school world and the real world. Dewey's wife, Alice Chipman, was also instrumental in grounding Dewey's sometimes ethereal concerns into the practical problems of the world, leading him to remark at her death, "My wife used to say quite truly that I go at things from the back end. I'm hampered by too much technical absorption" (retrieved from http://ns.umich.edu/MT/97/Sum97/mta1j97.html, November 20, 2010). It is no wonder, then, to realize that Dewey did not begin writing about issues in education and schooling until his wife and Addams began working on him in earnest and he had seen and experienced Hull House. In both Addams and Chipman, he had mentors on issues of education and social justice.

These two women, in many ways, set the stage for the contemporary emergence of "feminist pragmatism" that offers important extensions of the pragmatist ethos in relation to experience and education. Many of these theorists pick up on the pragmatist critique of the theory–practice divide, the notion of inter-subjectivity and the move away from Cartesian epistemology, and the role and importance of "lived experience" in knowledge claims. For example, Maxine Greene, in her classic *The Dialectic of Freedom* (1988, pp. 42–43), writes of men and women

> [m]aking more and more connections in their own experience, reflecting on their shared lives, taking heed of the consequences of the actions they performed, they would become aware of more and more alternatives, more and more experiential possibilities; and this meant an increased likelihood of achieving freedom.

Greene goes on to say that "the *person*—that center of choice—develops in his/her fullness to the degree he/she is a member of a live community" (p. 43, emphasis in text). Thus, while an individual is not subsumed underneath the social (there is still freedom to act), it is the degree to which experience is *shared* and acted upon collaboratively that makes it, in the end, worthwhile. As Hannah Arendt (1958) noted, "[n]o human life, not even the life of the hermit in nature's wilderness, is possible without a world which directly or indirectly testifies to the presence of other human beings" (p. 22).

Other feminist pragmatists have pushed the notion of experience further than Dewey, either through a more robust sense of "lived experience" and its importance in personal narratives, for example, or by criticizing Dewey's notion of experience as something outside of culture. Nel Noddings, for example, while a proponent of Deweyian notions of democratic living and experience, has trouble with Dewey's construction of moral conduct. To Noddings, locating experience within interaction and the social does not fully answer questions of power and justice embedded within social structures. She argues: "We know that Dewey will insist on locating the moral within the social (not in God, a special faculty, or established authority) . . . will 'the social' inevitably cast up criteria that are reliably moral, or must we mean by 'moral' whatever the social group establishes as normative?" (2006, pp. 74–75). Here we see how other voices within the pragmatist current push against the Deweyian notions of "growing" and "adaptation" with a more critical lens (something we'll explore in more detail in the next chapter). Through the lens of feminism, pragmatists like Noddings and Greene cannot help but see experience as *both* social *and* implicated in unequal relations of power. As Greene (1988) argues (pp. 8–9):

> The effects of early experience survive, along with the sedimentations of meaning left by encounters with a changing world. There are the effects of environment, class membership, economic status, physical limitations, as well as the impacts of exclusion and ideology. The growing, changing individual . . . always has to confront a certain weight in lived situations, if only the weight of memory and the past.

The "weight" of lived experience, here, is not automatically educative for Greene. Indeed, it can be oppressive. Experience can be woven through with issues of identity and power. While others (Kadlec 2007) have argued that Dewey was more aware of power and inequality than perhaps some feminist pragmatists (and others) have maintained, the attention contemporary pragmatists have brought to these issues is an important contribution to (and extension of) the main current. As Noddings (2006) writes: "Dewey has told us much more about the ethical conduct of education than about the ethical product. Like so many liberals of both yesterday and today, he puts enormous faith in right procedures. But will these procedures produce recognizable moral goods? That question still haunts us" (p. 82).

While there is much to celebrate and acknowledge in terms of both Dewey's legacy and the modern notions of interactive experience in pragmatism, it also comes with significant limitations. Some have critiqued the variation for being overly steeped in Enlightenment ideals of progress and a fetish for the scientific method. For example, Bowers (2003) sees such a legacy as offering no foundation for an ethical construction of experience in environmental education. Others see no evidence in Dewey of an awareness of marginalized groups in the democratic process. Indeed, as West (1989) notes, African-Americans are virtually invisible in Dewey's writing, and this leads one to ponder whose interests did Dewey see democracy serving in the end. Dewey and others who argue for a notion of democratic schooling seem to brush aside notions of power according to many of these criticisms. Diggins (1994), for example, is concerned that Deweyian democracy assumes a kind of homogeneous community that simply does not exist in a world of structural and institutional inequalities. Why, for example, do we assume that "people power" will automatically result in more just results? Certainly, at the most basic level, "mob rule" is an example of the limitations of "progress" through social experience. In the end, according to the critiques, the pragmatist construction of interactive experience is embedded in notions of social harmony, not conflict. Thus, the *process* of schooling (in both the formal and the informal curriculum) is viewed as adaptive and hopeful (and thus, progressive). Indeed, it will not be until the critical theory variation (discussed in Chapter 5) that we will see experience in education constructed as a site of struggle where questions of identity, power, and culture cannot be separated. These critiques are significant and remain a struggle for those who theorize within the pragmatist variation to reconcile as they attempt to argue that the underlying philosophy sets the stage for many of the modern progressive projects of today (Hewitt 2002; Kadlec 2007).

The Pragmatist Current in Experiential Education

So what curricular projects are made visible by this current in our river of experiential education? There is a wide variety, indicative of the influence and significance of this current in our river. To begin, as the quotation from Dewey at the beginning of this chapter reveals, the pragmatist current evokes curriculum projects where "shared experience . . . is the greatest of human goods." Within the field of experiential education, curricular models and programmatic approaches such as expeditionary learning, adventure education, challenge education, and service learning all place a great deal of importance on the value of shared, interactive experience. The very idea of an "expedition" which formed one of the nascent, core values of the field (through the work of Kurt Hahn and the establishment of Outward Bound) suggests the social and interactive nature of experience within this variation. Expeditions are completed by groups, typically, and not by individuals. Thoreau and Muir did not speak of "expeditions" as much as they did of "walks," "trips," and "journeys." These, of course, were most often solitary endeavors with the aim of encountering sublime and direct experiences individually. Indeed, even today, finding others on such trips ourselves often "ruins the experience" for us. By contrast, Expeditionary Learning (EL) schools are a relatively recent curriculum project developed by Outward Bound and an excellent example of the reinscription of experiential education toward more pragmatist orientations. For EL schools, the expedition happens within the school process. While this necessitates trips and time away from the classroom, it is not the sole purpose of the educational activity. The expedition takes on pedagogical weight in the ways in which experience is woven into the social activity of the school.

This notion of the sociality of experience plays into a second visible curricular project in experiential education—the conscious connection between the school and the community. Unlike the Romantic current where school life and learning were decoupled, in the pragmatist current they are wedded. Whitman's "Learn'd Astronomer" yielded little educational value. It is only when he rejects this formal education and wanders out alone that he claims some sense of illumination. To pragmatists, this is the very dichotomy that needs to be collapsed—the one that sets up a false distinction between the "real world" and the "school world." Rooted in the pragmatist epistemological claim about interactive experience, there is a constellation of experiential education curricula that views connecting school life and real life as the central aim of education. At its most extreme, this could take the form of "useful vocationalism" where students are tracked into "relevant" interests. Of course, this "social efficiency" form of educational pro-gressivism led to riots in New York city over the so-called "Gary Plan" (a progressive school reform program first adopted in the early twentieth century in Gary, Indiana) and continues today with those who are deeply critical of schooling organized around overly "practical" aims at the expense of more "academic" forms of learning. One has to put quotation marks around these terms as pragmatists would resist divorcing practical aims from academic ones. In their view, they ought to be one and the same.

Less extreme than vocational education are the myriad projects that aim to place learning into action in the community in which the school is located. Place-based education, for example, has arisen as a curriculum project that involves "the process of using the local community and environment as a starting point to teach concepts . . . this approach . . . helps students develop stronger ties to their community, enhances student appreciation for the natural world, and creates a heightened commitment to serving as active, contributing citizens" (Sobel, 2005, p. 7). In place-based education, curriculum is not lifted out of context and taught as a series of disconnected and detached facts-about-the-world but rather, as pragmatists would want, context becomes the center point. Instead of students in the Midwest of the United States learning about tropical rainforests in Peru, they might learn about the history of land-use in their bio-region and how that history informed the development of their town and the current challenges and opportunities it faces. They might talk with farmers, visit City Hall and learn about current problems, and perhaps also spend some time in the local river, doing water quality monitoring and natural history lessons. Such an education is much more than a couple of break-the-monotony-of-the-school-week field trips. Done seriously, it asks very tough questions about the purposes of schooling and what knowledge is of the most worth. To Gruenewald (2003): "[o]nce one begins to appreciate the pedagogical power of places, it is difficult to accept institutional discourses, structures, pedagogies, and curriculums that neglect them" (p. 641).

A third area made visible through the social construction of experience is the sense that experience forms the genesis of social action. Service learning, for example, is a rapidly emerging curriculum project in both K-12 (primary through secondary schooling) and higher education that seeks to purposefully link curricular and co-curricular learning. Just the switch from "extra-" curricular to "co-" curricular points to the pragmatist influence on this construction of educative experience. Learning outside the classroom is not, in this view, "extra." Rather, it ought to be woven into what we describe as academic or intellectual activity from the beginning. Really, like place-based education, service learning taken to its logical extreme would call all learning, both in and out of the classroom, "curricular" with no modifiers needed. Building a Habitat for Humanity house, cleaning up a polluted stream, or volunteering at the local Food Pantry cannot help but link the student to his or her community in crucial ways. Perhaps even more importantly, service learning, done well, moves beyond "mere volunteerism" to a critical consideration of the world-as-it-is and the world-as-it-should-be. Why is there hunger in my community? Who polluted this river? How do I make a difference in this world? This, more ethical slant to educative experience is an important component of some curricular projects in experiential education and it links directly back to Deweyian notions of democratic schooling. As Jay (2005) reiterates (p. 296):

> Beyond a mere political arrangement, democracy also has social and moral dimensions . . . to further this cause, Dewey argued, education for democracy was an absolute necessity. Such education must be based on experiential rather than book learning, creative investigation rather than rote memory, and a transactional relationship between a child and environment rather than a passive, spectatorial one.

The purpose of education and of experience in this social current is to *live* it in a shared sense. This continuous interaction between the self and society, between the past, present, and future, and between thinking and doing, is then both epistemological and ethical. It is epistemological because it makes claims on how we come to know about the world. It is ethical because it suggests that the knowing and the doing are transactional *in community*. How do we decide on right courses of action? By acting and thinking together. And democratic living entails creating spaces in which such acting and thinking can be done freely, publicly, and conjointly. To Dewey (1916) (p. 99):

> An undesirable society . . . is one which internally and externally sets up barriers to free intercourse and communication of experience. A society which makes provision for participation in its good of all its members on equal terms and which secures flexible readjustment of its institutions through interaction of the different forms of associated life is in so far democratic.

Deb Meier (1995), James Beane (1997), Ted Sizer (1997), Parker Palmer (2007), and Robert Fried (2001) all speak to the connections between experience and democracy in schools. As Beane argues, "a national curriculum should bring young people together to experience democracy and the democratic way of life. This means learning to work together on issues of shared concern" (1997, p. 92).

It is interesting to note that within some curriculum projects in the field of experiential education, these ethical connections are less prevalent. Why might this be the case? This current is *informed by* pragmatist philosophy but that does not mean it embodies it in all of its facets. And, as some have argued, perhaps Deweyian notions of experience are insufficiently critical. Perhaps some elements have become lost in translation. While the visible projects in this current in experiential education emphasize the social aspects of experience, some have not extended this as forcefully as they could into ideas of citizenship, community, and democracy. This may be due to the more applied orientation of a still developing field. But it may also signal to a deeper concern (picked up by those who argue from a more critical stance) that the emphasis on adaptation and change leaves this variation incapable of forceful normative goals. Regardless, it is clear that, for Dewey and other educational theorists within this current, democratic schooling and experience are inseparable notions. Thus, it remains an unfinished project of this current of experiential education to explore these connections to their fullest extent.

Conclusion

As we leave this current of experience, what have we learned? Certainly, our interactions with its character and flow have helped us realize that experience can be put to different uses from those revealed in the Romantic current. We learned that experience is not just an individual phenomena, it can also have a shared, social element that asks different questions and demands different educational responses from those we might have previously considered. It is one of the strongest currents in our river and we see this in the many ways social experience is lifted up in a variety of curricular projects in experiential education including adventure education, challenge education, place-based learning, and service learning to name just a few. And, we discovered that shot through this notion of "democratic schooling" are some very sticky questions about power, equality, and justice that remain unresolved in many respects. Is a social construction of experience automatically liberating and democratic? If there are no foundational truths in pragmatic thought, how do we arbitrate between conflicting individual and social aims? How does democratic living intersect with issues of inequality and interlocking oppressions? It is perhaps no surprise that leaving this current also means we carry with us unresolved questions and tensions. Each current will do that. No one current can ask or answer the totality of questions brought about by this notion of experience and education. But hopefully, as we explore, we continue to layer on our own more full understanding of experiential education and its myriad personalities.

5

EXPERIENCE AND THE POLITICAL

The Critical Current

It is when culture is "enlivened with organization," when it is educative, that it becomes, at least embryonically, hegemonic.

Antonio Gramsci

Introduction

A third current runs through the river of experience we have been exploring. It is perhaps the smallest current in our river, a thin line that exists on the edges and eddies and often runs counter to the main currents. It is also, relatively speaking, the most recent of the influential currents in experiential education. I have labeled this distinctive current with the title "Experience and the Political" to signal the ways in which experience in this variation is embedded within the dynamics of *power and social justice*. "Political," in this sense, does not refer to the domain of government but rather to the ways in which we might examine how power influences and dictates interactions and decision-making. Rather than viewing experience as a form of associated living and interaction as informed by the pragmatist current, or as individual meaning-making and transformation as informed by the Romantic current, the political current views experience through the lens of power, either as a tool for reproducing inequalities or as a means for emancipation (Reynolds, 1999). If the main currents in our river of experiential education are comprised of the romantic and pragmatist constructions of experience, the political current seems to be more of a counter-current. It often runs against the main flow and suggests aims and purposes of experience in education far different from much of the water we have explored up to this point. Yet, despite its relative size and impact, it must be accounted for. As any river person will tell you, the eddies and counter-currents are ignored at your peril.

Miss the counter-current and you might find yourself in the drink. As a fisherman and a gardener, I always try to pay attention to the "edge" or "boundary" effects—places where elements come together and interact. These are often the most dynamic and the ones with the most life and productivity. For these reasons, it's worth a journey through this distinctive counter-current.

In this chapter, as we have done in the previous two, we will first explore the historical context from which this particular current emerges, focusing in particular on how early theorists formed a new and distinctive notion of experience. In doing so, we will wade into the main ideas and key philosophical tenets of "critical theory" and what became known as the "Frankfurt School" in early twentieth-century Germany. Like our previous discussions regarding Romanticism and pragmatism, the work of the Frankfurt School should not be viewed as a single monolithic stance on experience. There were key distinctions and points of disagreement between the key figures in the movement as well as substantial changes in position by certain individuals at different times in their careers. Nonetheless, we can safely make the claim that the philosophical orientations that generally describe the Frankfurt theorists represent a distinctive shift from the approaches we have explored thus far. Following from this backdrop, we will examine the ways such a construction of experience informs views on education and schooling processes through the emergence of the field of critical pedagogy and the work of Paulo Freire in particular. Along the way, we will compare and contrast this construction of experience in our river of experiential education with the two discussed in the previous two chapters. We will then turn to a discussion of how this distinctive current forms a particular construction of experience as it is (or could be) employed within the field of experiential education. I use the phrase "could be" here as this current (along with post-structural orientations) is the least emphasized stance on experience employed at present within the field of experiential education. That being said, on the basis of recent scholarship, it is a growing area within the field (Breunig, 2005; Gruenewald, 2003; Roberts, 2005). Finally, we will conclude with a discussion of some of the possibilities and limitations of this current in the field of experiential education.

The Frankfurt School and the Crisis of Experience

Arising in Germany in the early to mid-twentieth century, a group of philosophers and social critics emerged in Europe who attempted to make sense of the emerging zeitgeist that saw the "failure" of Marxist theory and the ascendancy of capitalism as a global economic power. Walter Benjamin, Max Horkheimer, Herbert Marcuse, and Theodor Adorno were among those theorists who became known as the loosely affiliated "Frankfurt School" in Germany. Writing within a remarkable historical context (the rise of capitalism, communism, Nazism, and the social labor movement), the early Frankfurt School organized their work around several resonant themes: critiques of positivism, mass culture, and capitalism and the desire for social change. In essence, Frankfurt School theorists were attempting to explain how it was that, despite Marx's accurate predictions about the economic consequences of capitalism, the proletariat class *of* itself never became a class *for* itself. While the "facts on the ground" indicated that the rise of capitalism led to increased disparities in wealth and power, working-class individuals in Western Europe seemed incapable of "seeing" the oppressive structures around them. And, because they could not perceive such systemic conditions, they lacked a shared sense of struggle—they could not achieve solidarity or be a class *for* themselves. Where, Frankfurt theorists wondered, was the revolution?

In order to answer this, theorists such as Horkheimer, Marcuse, and Adorno looked to the concept of distortion. What prevents someone from seeing clearly? Something must function to *distort* an individual's perception about the world. The Frankfurt School took a much greater interest in the concept of distortion and the ways in which power, ideology, and politics permeate our analyses of the social world. To these theorists, the social sciences were not equivalent to the natural sciences in that the facts on the ground do not "speak for themselves." Rather, in the social sciences, we actively shape the gathering and analysis of said facts. As Horkheimer noted: "The facts which our senses present to us are socially performed in two ways: through the historical character of the object perceived and through the historical character of the perceiving organ. Both are not simply natural; they are shaped by human activity, and yet the individual perceives himself as receptive and passive in the act of perception" (1976, p. 213). This concept of the "shaping" of perception is key to understanding how this political current in our river shifts us in dramatic ways from the currents previously considered. And key to this shift is the concept of experience.

The quotation from Antonio Gramsci that begins this chapter sets the stage for the active shaping of perception. Gramsci notes that when culture becomes "educative" it has the potential to become "hegemonic." An awkward academic term, "hegemony" refers to a sense of ideological power exerted by a dominant group in a social setting. What is most revealing about hegemony in this sense is its potential to wield power not by material force but through the active shaping of perception through other means (economic, cultural, and ideological) and that this shaping is often not overtly perceived by those who are marginalized. A simple example might suffice. We know, for example, that young women in the United States are particularly prone to eating disorders such as anorexia and bulimia. These are terrible conditions that the women themselves, if they were thinking "rationally," would never subject themselves to. So how does it happen? From the theoretical orientation of the Frankfurt School, this form of oppression happens through the reproduction of images in the media and other cultural forms of communication (what Frankfurt theorists refer to as the "culture industry") that normalize a female body type of a particular shape and size (and one that only a minuscule percentage of women "naturally" have). Without realizing it, young women internalize these images and become the instruments of their own oppression by forcing themselves to look like the images they see as "normal." This is how culture becomes "educative" in the Gramscian sense and, thus, hegemonic. This shaping is not innocent. It functions to reproduce power and institutionalize inequality (in this case, patriarchy).

What does this have to do with our exploration of experiential education? By taking the stance that social institutions such as education can be vulnerable to "distortion" and hegemonic forces, this current marks an important break from the two currents discussed previously. In both the experience-as-social and the experience-as-individual currents, educative experience is seen as relatively neutral or hopeful. While both variations find fault with "traditional" schooling processes to one extent or another, they don't view these faults systemically. As Benton & Craib (2001) note in relation to social theory before the Frankfurt School "all [previous] approaches recognize that people can be wrong in their perceptions and conceptions of the social world but not that they can be systematically mistaken or misled by the type of society in which they live" (p. 111). In other words, the faith in the ameliorative worth of social experience for pragmatists or the transformative potential of authentic experience for romanticists both fail to account for the ways in which distortion operates in society. To the Frankfurt theorists, each of these constructions views educative experience as essentially incorruptible by the structural inequality evident in social relations. How might it change our notions of experience if we were to accept the idea that an individual may be *incapable* of genuine and reasoned reflection due to the ways in which distortion operates in society?

Fundamental to this theoretical orientation is a deep distrust of the educative power of "individual experience." Many in the Frankfurt School witnessed the power of propaganda, for example in the rise of Nazi Germany. Adorno, as he experienced the manipulation of the media and the public during World War II, seemed to grow increasingly cynical. He noted:

> The total obliteration of the war by information, propaganda commentaries, with cameramen in the first tanks and war reporters dying heroic deaths, the mishmash of enlightened manipulation of public opinion and oblivious activity: all this is another expression for the withering of experience, the vacuum between men and their fate, in which their real fate lies.
>
> *quoted in Jay, 2005, p. 345*

To Adorno, this withering of experience led to a deeply cynical and dark view on human potential. What could be claimed as individual experience any more when the power of the State to manipulate, to frame, to define, had seemingly become totalizing and all-encompassing? In many respects, this "death of experience" was the logical extension of the Frankfurt School's notion of distortion. In a world of propaganda, manipulation, and "false consciousness," experience itself, that most personal and seemingly "authentic" phenomenon, could no longer be trusted.

In another context, this theoretical orientation can be compared to the popular sci-fi movie series *The Matrix*. In this apocalyptic future world, the vast majority of the planet's population lives a lie. Machines actually rule the world, harvesting humans for energy, all the while generating a virtual thought-world for their subjects so that they may continue to be deluded into thinking that they are actually "free." In one memorable scene, one character, the ironically named "Mr. Reagan," meets with the antagonist, "Cypher" and agrees to become a double agent. As he digs into a free steak dinner provided to him by way of a bribe he observes, "I know this steak doesn't exist. I know that by putting it in my mouth the Matrix is telling me that it is juicy and delicious. After nine years do you know what I realize? [Takes large bite of steak] Ignorance is bliss." This is truly the dystopian future of the death of experience—when something so personal an experience as taste becomes a mirage, a mechanism for enslavement and oppression—and the public willingly accedes to such ignorance. As Jay noted, "[a]ttempts to revive a robust variety of experience in the present, Adorno would moreover argue, are doomed to failure, especially when they seek to recover a purported *ur*-experience that is somehow deeper that the mediations of culture and society" (2005, p. 346). Adorno himself argued that experience had been "replaced by the selective, disconnected, interchangeable and ephemeral state of being informed which, as one can already observe, will promptly be cancelled by other information" (quoted in Jay, 2005, p. 346). It is here that we can see the primary influence of the Frankfurt School on our construction of experience—it simply cannot "speak for itself" given the conditions of modernity.

Critical Theory

Yet, with the possible exception of Adorno, most Frankfurt theorists were not abject cynics and pessimists. They still held out some hope for social change and thus they often had conflicting and ambivalent views on what experience might be able to do for both the individual and society. Walter Benjamin, for example, wrote a letter to Theodor Adorno in 1940 about an early childhood memory that reveals this ambivalence:

> The roots of my "theory of experience" can be traced back to a childhood memory. My parents would go on walks with us, as a matter of course, wherever we spent the summer months. There would always be two or three of us children together. But it is my brother I am thinking of here. After we had visited one or other of the obligatory places around Freudenstadt, Wengen or Schreiberhau, my brother used to say, "Now we can say we've been there." This remark imprinted itself unforgettably on my mind.
>
> *quoted in Jay, 2005, p. 313*

In this passage, Benjamin recalls that his brother, upon seeing one of these places, declares that "Now we can say we've been there." The story is revealing in the ways in which Benjamin seems to play with the role of experience. Clearly, Benjamin is suggesting that there is something disturbing about a form of experience that is, in a sense, trivial and fleeting. But, in adding that this remark from his brother "imprinted itself unforgettably on my mind" he also seems to be signaling that there is something real to experience and its relationship to memory.

To understand this tension, we must wade into the dominant mode of analysis developed by the Frankfurt School and what is the school's most lasting legacy: critical theory. Critical theory might generally be defined as a form of politically aware social critique. Remember that Frankfurt School theorists wanted to show that "the world that you see is not the world that is." The world you "see" is a distorted world—a world shaped by others through forms of hegemonic power— what is often referred to as "false consciousness." So how might one cut through the distortion and truly "see"? Marx believed this form of seeing or class-consciousness would be inevitable as the proletariat became a class "for them-selves" in solidarity. But, as we mentioned earlier, this did not happen. Frankfurt theorists, in attempting to explain this through the concept of distortion, needed a way out of this Weberian "iron cage" (how the German sociologist Max Weber. whom we shall meet again later, described the inexorable increase in rational-ization in social organization). After all, simply accepting the "death of experi-ence" left one with no sense of agency, no form of individual and social action toward change and, eventual, emancipation. Critical theory was their answer.

Much more than a loose equation with "critical thinking," critical theory in this sense is best described by Stephen White's (2004) two-commitment minimum. As Kadlec (2007) recounts White's definition, "[a]ny genuinely critical theory or research tradition will, according to White, 1) cultivate a 'hermeneutics of suspicion' and 2) view 'social structures of inequality' as manifestations of power relations" (p. 14). Cultivating a "hermeneutics of suspicion" allows one to check lived experience against one's understanding of how that experience might be shaped and framed by larger socio-cultural forces. To White, key to this stance was a deep awareness of how perceived inequalities are the functions of power relations. So, to return to our example of Benjamin's letter to Adorno: remember that he noted that the roots of his "theory of experience" came from his brother remarking that "Now we can say we've been there" upon visiting one tourist spot or another, and that Benjamin wrote that "This remark imprinted itself unforgettably on my mind." Benjamin is suggesting that experiences can be fleeting, distorted, and consumerist in orientation (e.g. Benjamin's brother's remark), but they can also be deeply educative if approached with the right frame of mind. Benjamin noted how "unforgettable" this remark was for him. Why? He does not say. But we can surmise that it is because he now "sees" experience differently and thus, his brother's remark takes on an educative aspect it might not have had otherwise. Thus, the tension is that, for critical theorists, experience *can* be viewed as a form of false consciousness but that is not to say experience is *only* a social construct without any basis in the material world or individuals' everyday lives. Experience might just as well be used to cut through the distortion and see how the world can be hegemonic. But how might one cultivate this sensibility? This question inevitably points to education and schooling and to the development of the field of critical pedagogy.

Critical Pedagogy: Critical Theory and Education

To actively resist distortion and maintain White's "two-commitment" minimum for what it means to be critical, some form of educative process must be put into place. Yet, as the Frankfurt School theorists argued, Rousseau's hands-off approach to schooling and Dewey's faith in the democratic classroom would each still result in forms of false consciousness. The individual, on her own, could not be trusted to achieve critical sensibilities. The machinations of the culture industry were simply too strong. Nor could the school, as currently organized, be trusted to educate for critical reasoning. In fact, critical theorists believe that current school processes are designed to achieve the exact opposite—to legitimate and reproduce the current, unequal, status quo. As Apple (2004) states: "schools may not be geared to select and produce neutrally a 'diversely skilled and qualified work force.' Rather, they seem to be less concerned with the distribution of skills than they are with the distribution of norms and dispositions which are suitable to one's place in a hierarchical society" (p. 17). From the lens of critical theory, schooling, as a social institution fundamentally shaped by capitalist ideology, functions as a mechanism for social reproduction, not social transformation. It is, in fact, its central purpose to control "both the knowledge preserving and know-ledge producing institutions of a particular society" (p. 25). So, if we are to attempt to resist the cultural processes of false consciousness, distortion, and hegemony, how are we to learn to do so if we cannot rely on either ourselves or our schools as they are currently constituted?

The answer was to invent a new form of education, critical pedagogy, and organize the curriculum around a singular purpose—the notion of critical consciousness. Ira Shor, in *Empowering Education* (1992), defined critical pedagogy as (p. 129):

> Habits of thought, reading, writing, and speaking which go beneath surface meaning, first impressions, dominant myths, official pronouncements, traditional clichés, received wisdom, and mere opinions, to understand the deep meaning, root causes, social context, ideology, and personal conse-quences of any action, event, object, process, organization, experience, text, subject matter, policy, mass media, or discourse.

Notice here that Shor's definition cuts right to the heart of the Frankfurt theorists' concern with distortion. This new form of education would be "empowering" because it would go beneath "surface meaning" and "received wisdom" to gain critical understanding. Importantly, Shor implicates not only texts, subject matter, and the media in his definition but *experience* as well. Experience, too, must be interrogated as to how it might function to reproduce inequalities and false consciousness. In this view, to "think critically" goes far beyond the taken-for-granted notions of the term often championed in schools. Thinking critically does not simply entail a general "intellectual constitution." Rather, to advocates of critical pedagogy, it is a penetrating and all-encompassing stance toward the world. It seeks to make ideologies, distortions, and hegemony overt and visible, and, in doing so, to suggest how we might imagine a world otherwise. As Breunig (2008) recounts, "this form of critical pedagogy is a way of thinking about, negotiating, and transforming the relationship among classroom teaching, the production of knowledge, the institutional structures of school, and the social and material relation to the wider community" (p. 471). But what does this look like pedagogically? How does a notion of experience in education become practiced out as critical pedagogy? The figure perhaps best known for developing the foundations of critical pedagogy is Paulo Freire. It is worth wading in to Freire's work here to gain specificity as to how this approach relates to our exploration of experiential education.

Freire's Critical Experience

It has been argued that Paulo Freire is a "father-figure" of critical theory in education (Breunig, 2008; McLaren, 1998). In many ways, if Dewey forms one of the cornerstones of the experience-as-social variation in experiential education, Freire is clearly his counterpart in the experience-as-political current discussed here.[1] Freire's life and work are the subject of countless volumes and well beyond the scope of this particular project. Of most direct use to us is the way in which Freire helped shape a new notion of the role of experience in the educational process, and it is this contribution that we will focus on here.

The impact of Freire on how we think about the social institution of schooling and the informal curricular process of socialization cannot be over-estimated. His seminal text, *Pedagogy of the Oppressed* (1970), is one of the single most cited works

---

1   The patriarchal orientation of this history should be noted. Until quite recently, "subaltern" voices in experiential education have not been acknowledged. The traditional intellectual lineage of John Dewey, Kurt Hahn, and Paulo Freire, for example, remains the foundational approach. This, of course, ignores the work of important voices such as Dorothy Lee (1986), bell hooks (1994), and Patricia Hill Collins (2000), to name a few of the more prominent educators and theorists who intersect on issues of experience and education.

in the literature on education and schooling. It is here that the broader critical theory becomes actualized as the educational stance of critical pedagogy. As McLaren (1998) writes (p. 186):

> A major task of critical pedagogy has been to disclose and challenge the role that schools play in our political and cultural life . . . critical [pedagogists] generally analyze schools in a twofold way: as sorting mechanisms in which select groups of students are favored on the basis of race, class, and gender; and as agencies for self and social empowerment . . . [They] argue that teachers must understand the role that schooling plays in joining knowledge and power, in order to use that role for the development of critical and active citizens.

This joining of knowledge with power is a strong theme in Freire's work and comes out strongly in *Pedagogy of the Oppressed*. In describing his "banking theory" of education, Freire dismisses the assumed neutrality of "mere facts" and illuminates how knowledge acquisition is tied to larger cultural processes. Freire (1970, p. 72) notes that:

> in the banking concept of education, knowledge is a gift bestowed by those who consider themselves knowledgeable upon those whom they consider to know nothing. Projecting an absolute ignorance on to others, a characteristic of the ideology of oppression, negates education and knowledge as processes of inquiry.

To Freire, experience, as a form of knowledge, becomes implicated in the same hegemonic processes as other forms of knowledge. In the banking concept of education, "experience" becomes something defined and owned by the knowledge producers. As an ultimately conservative orientation, experience is equated with accumulated wisdom, something students must learn *from* their teachers and not something *lived* or enacted. This recalls the German etymological distinction between *Erfahrung* (accumulated experience) and *Erlebnis* (lived experience) we highlighted in Chapter 1. To Freire, quoting Eric Fromm, banking education promotes "necrophily" rather than "biophily." Fromm's use of experience and wisdom in the following passage cited by Freire in *Pedagogy of the Oppressed* is particularly revealing.

> While life is characterized by growth in a structured, functional manner, the necrophilous person loves all that does not grow, all that is mechanical. The necrophilous person is driven by the desire to transform the organic into the in-organic, to approach life mechanically, as if all living persons were things . . . *Memory, rather than experience; having rather than being, is what counts.*
> *Fromm, quoted in Freire, 1970, p. 77, emphasis added*

Freire goes on to note that oppression and the need for control are necrophilous and that the banking model of education transforms students into receivers of knowledge rather than experiencing the power of their own ideas.

Thus, in hegemonic schooling situations, experience becomes a tool of oppression, "changing the consciousness" of the oppressed by devaluing their everyday lived experience and replacing it with a banking model of education. McLaren (1998) summarizes this stance well (p. 203):

> The dominant culture is able to "frame" the ways in which subordinate groups live and respond to their own cultural system and lived experiences; in other words, the dominant culture is able to manufacture dreams and desires for both dominant and subordinate groups by supplying "terms of reference" (i.e. images, visions, stories, ideals) against which all individuals are expected to live their lives.

Such structural inequality has the ability to produce "false consciousness" within both the oppressed and the oppressor. As a result, we cannot automatically rely on the transformative and ameliorative power of experience to emancipate us from inequality. Indeed, experience itself might be implicated in maintaining "false" consciousness. As bell hooks (1994) details in her chapter "Essentialism and Experience" in *Teaching to Transgress*: "the very discursive practices that allow for the assertion of 'the authority of experience' have already been determined by a politics of race, sex, and class domination" (p. 81).

So, is there a way out of this oppressive system? To Freire, the answer lay in developing a "problem-posing" style of education as a counter to the banking model. In this "dialogic" mode of communication, both the student and teacher engage in a communication form that is transactional. "Through dialogue, the teacher-of-the-students and the students-of-the-teacher cease to exist and a new term emerges: teacher-student with student-teachers" (Freire, 1970, p. 80). According to Freire, such an approach does not dichotomize cognition and experience the way the banking system tends to by suggesting that experience only comes at the end of the day. In the problem-posing approach, experience is brought into the dialogue as a living and organic aspect of the classroom and links the "classroom world" with the "real world" collapsing the false dichotomy in a way Dewey would likely approve. For critical pedagogues, this is what is meant by "praxis"—a conscious linking of thinking and acting upon the world that points a way out of a hegemonic state toward liberation. To Freire "[a]uthentic liberation—the process of humanization—is not another deposit to be made in men. Liberation is a praxis: the action and reflection of men and women upon their world in order to transform it" (1970, p. 79). Thus, to Freire and others in this current of experience, the central aim of education is not a homogeneous form of associated living and social harmony as pragmatists sometimes argue, or a more individual and/or transcendent self-actualization as the Romantic current might emphasize. Rather, the purpose of schooling is a kind of critical conscious-ness that attempts to reveal structural and systemic inequality while also providing a sense of urgency to act locally on these injustices.

Thus, the experience-as-political current locates the individual as an active agent of change. But, unlike the experience-as-individual current, the change is not located within the individual but rather connects the individual to larger social forces through the idea of praxis. Transformation, in this sense, is *both* individual and societal in the sense that the individual is given tools of awareness to see through the distortion and act out in the world in a different way. To Freire (1970, p. 51):

> One of the gravest obstacles to the achievement of liberation is that oppressive reality absorbs those within it and thereby acts to submerge human beings' consiousness [*sic*]. Functionally, oppression is domesticating. To no longer be prey to its force, one must emerge from it and turn upon it. This can be done only by means of praxis: reflection and action upon the world in order to transform it.

Within the experience-as-political current, experience is constructed within a broader milieu of structural inequality. Individual experience can be *both* oppressive *and* liberating depending upon how it is employed within the educational process. This connects to Giroux's notion of the theory of interest and the theory of experience within critical pedagogy (McLaren, 1998). McLaren notes that "by theory of interest, Giroux means that curriculum reflects the interests that surround it . . . By theory of experience, Giroux means that curriculum is an historically constructed narrative that produces and organizes student experiences" (p. 191). Thus the individual, within this current, can be shaped by experience through a historically constructed narrative. In this form, experience is potentially oppressive to the individual. It recalls Ray McDermott's (1987) haunting line that "[f]ailure is waiting every morning in every classroom in the United States. Before children or their teachers arrive, failure is there" (p. 130). In this analysis, it is *experience* that waits for children, already existing prior to the educational moment. But, rather than such a construction being totalizing and overdeterministic, experience within this construction *also* has the potential to be liberating through dialogue and praxis—essentially writing a new narrative of freedom and power.

Beyond Freire: Possibilities and Limitations

While Freire is clearly the foundational voice on matters of experience and education in critical pedagogy, he is by no means the end of the story. As others have attempted to put these ideas into practice, the possibilities and limitations of this construction of experience in education have become clearer. For example, Macedo (2000) argues in the introduction to *Pedagogy of the Oppressed* (p. 17):

Unfortunately in the United States, many educators who claim to be Freirean in their pedagogical orientation mistakenly transform Freire's notion of dialogue into a method, thus losing sight of the fact that the fundamental goal of dialogical teaching is to create a process of learning and knowing that invariably involves theorizing about the experiences shared in the dialogue process. Some strands of critical pedagogy engage in an overdose of experiential celebration that offers a reductionistic view of identity . . . such pedagogy leaves identity and experience removed from the problematics of power, agency, and history.

Macedo's concern here of "an overdose of experiential celebration" points directly to a potential limitation in this construction of experience. By emphasizing dialogue and student voice, educators may cede too much authority. Authority, it should be noted, comes from "authorship" or, generally, expressions of "voice." Too much emphasis on a form of personal narrative and expression of lived experience without a deeper form of dialogue and interrogation of said experiences may not be liberatory at all. In fact, it might function to reproduce existing dynamics of power. As Macedo continues (emphasis added, p. 18):

By overindulging in the legacy and importance of their respective voices and experiences, these educators often fail to move beyond a notion of difference structured in polarizing binarisms and uncritical appeals to the discourse of experience. I believe that it is for this reason that some of these educators invoke *a romantic pedagogical mode that "exoticizes" discussing lived experiences as a process of coming to voice.*

Countering this perceived limitation, though, is bell hooks's vigorous defense of personal student voice in her chapter, "Essentialism and Experience" in *Teaching to Transgress*. In this chapter, hooks directly addresses the criticism (articulated in Diana Fuss, 1989) that allowing students to discuss personal experience in the classroom is somehow "soft" pedagogy. hooks (1994) argues (p. 89):

Identity politics emerges out of the struggles of oppressed or exploited groups to have a standpoint on which to critique dominant structures, a position that gives purpose and meaning to struggle. Critical pedagogies of liberation respond to these concerns and necessarily embrace experience, confessions and testimony as relevant ways of knowing, as important, vital dimensions of any learning process.

To hooks, the use of lived experiences in classrooms, through processes such as personal narratives, is not "romantic" as Macedo and Fuss argue, it is central to the struggle for a reclaimed sense of identity in educational institutions that function to marginalize and disempower certain ways of knowing and being in the world.

hooks further articulates this strategic pedagogy as tapping into the "passion of experience." In order for a teacher to occupy a privileged position, that is, one that combines both analytical and experiential ways of knowing, she must have lived through the "passion of experience, the passion of remembrance" (1994, p. 90). This is quite different from a teacher or student using the "authority of experience." When students see the passion of experience modeled and are able to practice it in the classrooms themselves, hooks believes there is a far greater likelihood of students experiencing education as the practice of freedom. She claims, "when I use the phrase 'passion of experience,' it encompasses many feelings but particularly suffering, for there is a particular knowledge that comes from suffering. It is a way of knowing that is often expressed through the body, what it knows, what has been deeply inscribed on it through experience" (p. 91). This extension of lived experience to the notion of embodied suffering reclaims experience from Adorno's distorted "death" to something that can be used for personal empowerment and, with hope, societal transformation.

This claim within critical pedagogy has its critics, however. Ellsworth (1989) for example, argued in her classic essay "Why Doesn't This Feel Empowering?" that critical pedagogy employs a variety of "repressive myths" that function to reproduce inequalities rather than transcend them. Ellsworth notes that critical pedagogues themselves do not exist "outside" of language, history, and power. Why should we trust the teacher, employing critical pedagogy, to somehow "rise above" structural inequalities?

> By this I mean that when participants in our class attempted to put into practice prescriptions offered in the literature concerning empowerment, student voice, and dialogue, we produced results that were not only unhelpful, but actually exacerbated the very conditions we were trying to work against, including Eurocentrism, racism, sexism, classism, and 'banking education.'"
>
> *Ellsworth, 1998, p. 298*

Ellsworth, from her post-structural and feminist leanings, finds significant problems in a pedagogical approach that claims to know the way out of hegemonic relations. She cites Trinh Minh-ha, who states, "There are no social positions exempt from becoming oppressive to others . . . any group—any position—can move into the oppressor role" (p. 322). The notion that experiential education, employed through critical pedagogy, will lead to more empowered relations is worth troubling. For example, a colleague once told me of a mandatory service learning experience at a local university. Members of a sorority took a trip down to an urban redevelopment zone in a major metropolitan city in an effort to help revitalize a "blighted" neighborhood. While at the job site, two members of the class posed for a photo and encouraged a third to "take a picture of us, this is *so* ghetto!" Clearly, these students were "coming to voice" and engaging in "experiential" activity with a purported social justice theme, but was it the kind of transformative education Freire envisioned? Indeed, experience as praxis, done *poorly*, can be more damaging than maintaining more "traditional" curriculum orientations. Shor & Freire (1987) make this point when they refer to their image of an experiential educator, what they call a dialogical teacher: "dialogical experience which is not based in seriousness, in competency, is *much worse* than a banking experience where the teacher merely transfers knowledge" (p. 80, emphasis in text).

Beyond concerns about the aims of critical pedagogy, others have made issue with the tendency within the orientation to over-emphasize structural inequality. In attempting to question the innocence and neutrality of experience, critical pedagogues (despite seemingly knowing better) often resort to grand narratives of oppression and power that devalue the power of individual agency. As Delpit (1995) notes (p. 47):

> We must keep the perspective that people are experts on their own lives. There are certainly aspects of the outside world of which they might not be aware, but they can be the only authentic chroniclers of their own experience. We must not be too quick to deny their interpretations, or accuse them of "false consciousness."

If all one gets, from critical pedagogy, is a sense of doom and despair about the structural barriers that impede progress, it is difficult to see what concrete steps might be possible in making the world a better place. Worse, the skepticism that critical pedagogy encourages can yield a deep distrust of self and society, causing individuals to slide perhaps too easily into a spectatorial cynicism that precludes social action. In addition, the critical orientation to experience and education espoused by the proponents of this current seems to overlook the significance of the obstacles to its implementation. As Shor & Freire (1987) note, "[i]t would be tremendously naïve to ask the ruling class in power to put into practice a kind of education which can work against it" (p. 36). Ellsworth also claims, "while the literature states implicitly or explicitly that critical pedagogy is political, there have been no sustained research attempts to explore whether or how the practices it prescribes actually alter specific power relations outside or inside schools" (1989, p. 301). If experiential education is currently marginalized by the dominant modes of educational practice in schools today as most acknowledge that it is, what possible worth would there be in emphasizing its counter-hegemonic power? Pragmatic orientations might argue that this emphasis on conflict as opposed to harmony makes it difficult to see "hope" and the possibility of progress in schools and in larger democratic processes. While it can be debated, as with the experience-as-social current discussed in the previous chapter, that the problem with critical pedagogy is that it has not been faithfully applied, it is worth noting that such pronouncements mean little to the students experiencing this form of education in our schools. Whether or not the criticisms of critical pedagogy mentioned above are based upon "correct" versions of critical pedagogy or not, they are represented *as* critical pedagogy, and, as a result, implicate the overall approach. In the end, these possibilities and limitations, like those within the Romantic and pragmatist currents, remain important issues to wrestle with for those that find power and promise in the experience-as-political current.

Political Current in Experiential Education

Has this current taken hold in curriculum projects within experiential education? It is certainly true that, as critical pedagogy has gained currency and popularity in academe, many have claimed Freire and others (Apple, Giroux, McLaren) as intellectual allies. Within the field of experiential education, critical pedagogy has begun to appear with more regularity (Breunig, 2005; Fenwick, 2001; Reynolds, 1999; Roberts, 2005). But it is less clear whether the field of experiential education has really taken Freire's critical stance to heart or is simply appropriating useful "methods" into existing romantic or pragmatist structures. Does a more rigorous form of critical pedagogy play out in experiential curricula? It would be fair to say that it certainly is not the most prevalent current of experience employed in the field today. It can be argued that, to this point, the track records of some experiential education curriculum projects have been quite poor in relation to issues of race, gender, class, and other social justice issues. Through the work of Freire and others in critical pedagogy, the experience-as-political current offers a much stronger stance on social justice issues. Experience can, potentially, be employed toward counter-hegemonic aims. As McLaren noted, "critical educators argue that *praxis* (informed action) must be guided by *phronesis* (the disposition to act truly and rightly). This means, in critical terms, that actions and knowledge must be directed at eliminating pain, oppression, and inequality, and at promoting justice and freedom" (1998, p. 210). Thus, rather than simply dismissing the use of experiential education as inherently "bad," the experience-as-political current can, in the ideal, work with the racialized, gendered, and class-based nature of "experience" in order to move toward a more liberatory pedagogy. In this way, it openly politicizes experience. It first deconstructs its assumed neutrality and then seeks to employ it toward acts of resistance and liberation. Whether it's the intersection between experience and class, gender, race, sexual orientation, or various combinations of these identities, this current of experience reminds educators that we must wrestle with how various constructions of experience are formed, contested, amplified, and/or marginalized through both the formal and informal curriculum. For example, critical pedagogues might ask how we could use experience (through racial autobiographies, for example) to talk about white privilege. Breunig (2005) argues (p. 480):

> Asking students to write educational autobiographies to explore their experiences with schools and with learning represents one starting point to

this process. Encouraging students to share and discuss their autobiographies allows them an opportunity to better understand their various subjectivities and the differing educational experiences of students within the classroom . . . Asking students to read *White Privilege: Unpacking the Invisible Backpack* (McIntosh, 1989), and asking them to unpack their individual "backpack" of privilege allows them to name themselves and relate that to the dominant ideology, locating their "positionality" in relation to that ideology.

If experience, within the political current, is already gendered, racialized, and implicated in other forms of identity and power, then the educational task is to "make the invisible, visible" by naming it so. This is true both for student and teacher. As Breunig (2005) makes a point to note in relation to her role as an experiential educator who practices critical pedagogy: "I 'locate' myself as someone who is a product of the system" (p. 478).

Ivan Illich's classic and provocative speech in Cuernavaca, Mexico, in 1968, "To Hell with Good Intentions," is another example of this "naming" of power and privilege. In this speech to the Conference on InterAmerican Student Projects (CIASP), Illich criticizes seemingly "innocent" notions of service and mission work that do not take into account who is doing the service "to" whom and for what purpose. Illich notes:

> All you will do in a Mexican village is create disorder. At best, you can try to convince Mexican girls that they should marry a young man who is self-made, rich, a consumer, and as disrespectful of tradition as one of you. At worst, in your "community development" spirit you might create just enough problems to get someone shot after your vacation ends and you rush back to your middleclass neighborhoods where your friends make jokes about "spits" and "wetbacks." You start on your task without any training. Even the Peace Corps spends around $10,000 on each corps member to help him adapt to his new environment and to guard him against culture shock. How odd that nobody ever thought about spending money to educate poor Mexicans in order to prevent them from the culture shock of meeting you?
>
> *retrieved December 11, 2010, from http://www.swaraj.org/illich_hell.htm*

How different might service learning experiences be if, to begin, students read Illich's criticisms and then had an opportunity to discuss the implications to their planned efforts. Illich concludes his speech in his typically acerbic style: "I am here to challenge you to recognize your inability, your powerlessness and your incapacity to do the 'good' which you intended to do. I am here to entreat you to use your money, your status and your education to travel in Latin America. Come to look, come to climb our mountains, to enjoy our flowers. Come to study. But do not come to help." Whether or not one agrees with Illich (he is nothing if not provocative), "making visible" such innocent notions of service and experience is an essential component of experiential education from the standpoint of this current.

One final example comes from the field of critical geography. Place-based learning approaches, for example, often take on innocent or naive approaches to experience-in-place that begin from assumptions about the inherent "goodness" of local engagements such as adopt-a-stream programs, community gardens, or oral history projects. The result of this can be a form of romanticization of place that fails to account for the ways in which place, like experience, is not a neutral or innocent concept. Castell notes:

> Space is not a "reflection of society," it is society . . . Therefore spatial forms, at least on our planet, will be produced, as all other objects are, by human action. They will express and perform the interests of the dominant class according to the mode of production and to a specific mode of development. They will express and implement the power relationships of the state in an historically defined society.
>
> *quoted in Gruenewald, 2003, p. 628*

Environmental education that focuses on experiences-in-place often does so without sufficient attention to the ways in which places themselves are socially constructed and thus racialized, gendered, and classed. To Gruenewald: "educational treatments of place must be attentive to life on the margins . . . Learners might ask, for example: Where are the margins? How have they been constructed? How do they reveal not only multiple forms of oppression, but possibilities for resistance to and transformation of domination?" (pp. 632–633). Here again we see the possibilities of the experience-as-political current in experiential education. By recognizing the ways place-based education might employ rather innocent notions of experience in places, it can both critique *and* explore how a reinscribed sense of place creates possibilities for individual and social change.

Conclusion

It still remains to be seen how this current will play out in our river of experience. As I mentioned in the introduction to this chapter, the experience-as-political current is certainly the least emphasized and employed in experiential education. It is less clear whether this atrophied state is due to the relative newness of critical pedagogy in comparison to more pragmatic and romantic intellectual histories. If this were the case, we might expect a steady increase in both theoretical and practical educational projects evoking a notion of experience similar to what has been described in this chapter. Another possible explanation of the subaltern nature of this construction of experience in experiential education, however, is less hopeful. It may just be that the ideological foundations of the field of experiential education preclude a more political orientation. Steeped as it is in romantic notions of learning, incorporating the theoretical orientations above may simply run counter to the predominant currents that applying them would assure its general demise.

And perhaps, from the standpoint of this current, a rearticulation of experience is exactly what is necessary. Michael Shellenberger and Ted Nordhaus's (2005) essay "The Death of Environmentalism" makes a related point in relation to the environmental movement. In it, the authors criticize the ideological foundations of the current environmental movement and suggest that the only way forward is to "kill off" the current movement and rearticulate it. They claim that "[w]hat the environmental movement needs more than anything else right now is to take a collective step back and re-think everything" (p. 7). They go on to argue that, "[b]y failing to question their most basic assumptions about the problem and the solution, environmental leaders are like generals fighting the last war—in particular the war they fought and won for basic environmental protections more than 30 years ago" (p. 7). According to the authors, only by leaving the old assumptions behind can the environmental movement move forward in a way that is inclusive and truly progressive.

This may ring true for the field of experiential education as well. As critical theory infiltrates the field, more and more of the curriculum projects and foundational assumptions of experiential education come into question. How do we make the field more inclusive? What are the implications of curriculum projects built on white, middle-class values delivered to Others? What if the curriculum models we have assumed to be educative are, in fact, mis-educative? It may be in the end, from the standpoint of the political current, that experiential education as it is currently practiced has to "die" in order for a new orientation to emerge. At the very least, as Shellenberger and Nordhaus argue, our time wading into the experience-as-political current suggests that the field may have to take a collective step back and re-examine core assumptions. It is for these reasons that this current might properly be described as a counter-current. It runs against the main flow. But, as we found, such currents cannot be ignored. Their dynamism and productivity mark the edges where potential lies in waiting.

6

EXPERIENCE AND THE MARKET

The Normative Current

Freedom is only half of the story, half the truth. On its own, freedom is a negative concept that has to be complemented by its positive counterpart, responsibility, an awareness of being responsible. Freedom threatens to degenerate into arbitrariness or license if it is not lived in terms of responsibility.

Viktor Frankl (1985)

Introduction

The final current we will explore in our river of experience may, in fact, not be a "current" at all. Whereas our previous three notions of experience are employed more or less consciously within the field of experiential education, this last notion may be more of a *result* or consequence than a theoretical perspective. Perhaps the best way to explain its significance is to continue our metaphor. We have been considering the theoretical landscape of experiential education as a river with many currents—some larger, some smaller, some flowing in the same direction, some running counter to the "main" current. Our last notion of experience however, the one explored in this chapter, does not exist *within* the river but rather influences the river from the surrounding landscape. For example, one rising environmental concern relative to water systems is the phenomenon of "run-off." As we continue to hardscape our environment through parking lots, paved roads, and other non-permeable landscaping, rainwater, rather than soaking into the ground, runs off more rapidly into stream and river systems, creating "pulses" which contribute to flooding, erosion, and pollution in the water. In other words, activity away from the river affects the characteristics of the river itself. As this process increases, the river loses its character and the diversity of its

currents. Floodwaters cover over the smaller eddies, smooth over the rough sur-
faces, and reduce water clarity. While flooding is certainly a "natural" phenomenon, if it occurs too much, the personality and make up of a river changes.
Species that used to thrive in the old environment can no longer compete. Turns
and bends in the river straighten out. The river takes on a more homogeneous
feel. It is still a river, no doubt, but it is a changed river. In this chapter, we will
explore the nature of this phenomenon that has arguably changed the character
of our river and why it ought to be a concern for those interested in the role of
experience in democratic forms of education and schooling.

The label for this exploration, "Experience and the Market," signals the ways
in which the rise of market economies and a variation of rationalism has normalized a particular notion of experience in education. In exploring these
processes, we will be drawing from the work of Max Weber, Jürgen Habermas,
and George Ritzer as a way to ground the historical movement toward what
I will label "neo-experientialism." Weber's work in particular is critical to
illuminating two processes that are central to understanding how the construction
of experience has changed through the rise of market economies: modernization
and rationalization. We will first explore the meaning of these terms and then
proceed through the work of Habermas and Ritzer to discuss how such a
theoretical grounding helps illuminate the rise of neo-experientialism and its
association with the rise of the market. Moving from the theoretical landscape
around the river to the river itself, we will then examine how these processes have
affected education and, in particular, experiential education. Finally, several key
or defining characteristics of neo-experientialism will be explored in addition to
the normative consequences of such a construction of experience in education. I
will be using here two, different conceptions of what it means for something to
be "normative." In the first case, normative implies a process by which something
becomes the norm—a taken-for-granted "given" in a particular time and place.
In this sense, I will argue that neo-experientialism has become the taken-for-
granted norm when we consider experiential education. The second conception
of the term comes from ethics and means something entirely different. In this sense,
"normative" implies ethical considerations about how one "ought" to live or act—
what is referred to as "normative ethics." In this chapter we will also consider
normative questions—whether or not the neo-experiential current as it will be
conceptualized here is an ethical current—if it directs us in ways that we think it
"ought" to. This line of thinking will also carry us forward toward the concluding
chapter on experience and democracy and what I label as the "hopeful current."

Weber, Modernization, and Rationalization

It is beyond the scope of this project to explore, in any real depth, the full
theoretical work of Max Weber on social, political, and economic theory.
Nonetheless, Weber's contributions to the understanding of the processes of

modernity are central to the main thesis of this chapter: namely that the rise of market economies has dramatically altered how we come to think about experience in education. So, it is worth a brief foray into the elements of his work that are most salient to our exploration here. Importantly, and contrary to "straight" Marxist theory, Weber does not focus exclusively on the study of the economic processes of modernity. While he, like Marx, saw the importance of the relations of production, he sought to explain the cultural significance of those changes. This distinction is illustrated in Weber's classic work *The Protestant Ethic and the Spirit of Capitalism* (1930), where he "turned Marx on his head" by suggesting that material conditions alone cannot explain social phenomena. Rather, for Weber, there is an interplay between cultural structure and material production. In this, perhaps his most famous work, Weber attempts to explain a paradox—how a religious tradition (Protestantism) founded on the rejection of material pursuits and profiteering could become wedded to the rise of capitalism in Europe. As Dodd (1999) states (p. 37):

> Weber maintains that the unprecedentedly [*sic*] rational pursuit of profit in which the Calvinists engaged sprang from an emotional or psychological response to religious teaching: the pursuit of economic prosperity to glorify God and sustain an inner belief that one has been chosen. It was only later that the production of profit became an end in itself.

Dodd's last line here, that "it was only later that the production of profit became an end in itself," is critical to understanding how Weber frames the processes of modernization and rationalization. How is it that profit became an end in itself? To understand this shift, we must explore the distinction Weber makes between goal and value rationality.

Weber's sociological theory can best be understood as the study of "meaningful action as opposed to behavior" (Benton & Craib, 2001, p. 77). He was more interested in social interaction and how various players adjusted to conditions than he was in developing some functionalist theory. For example, while a bike rider is certainly engaging in action of a certain kind, it is not *social action*. If the bike rider crashes into another bike rider, that, still, is not *social* action as there was no intentionality and thus it is not yet *meaningful*. It is only in the ensuing argument between the two parties where the action is *meaningful* that action becomes *social action*. Weber (1947) lays out four different types of meaningful social action: traditional, affectual, value, and practical. It is in the last two of these types—value action and practical action—where Weber's normative[1] stance on modernity emerges. To Weber, traditional and affectual social action can be separated from value and practical action in the sense that "they are carried out primarily for the

---

1 Remember that "normative" as it is used here refers to normative ethics.

satisfaction they bring, not to achieve any other purpose in the world (Benton & Craib, 2001, p. 77). Traditional social action is action based on the fact that "we have always done it that way before." Affectual social action is action based upon emotion—for example, if one of the bike riders had gotten angry and took a swing at the other. In both of these cases, the social action is not properly rational in the sense that the action did not take into consideration consequences or broader social purposes.

The third meaningful form of social action, value actions, are those "oriented to ultimate values" (Benton & Craib, 2001, p. 77) and cannot, at first, be justified rationally. For example, according to Weber, a Christian cannot justify his or her faith rationally. However, once he or she acts in the world, by attending church, by praying, or adopting specific attitudes and behaviors, those actions could be considered rational as they are based upon on an ultimate value (his or her faith). Finally, practical action is that which is "directed toward concrete, achievable ends" (p. 78). Going to college or university, for example, is often justified on the grounds of practical rationality—that doing so will "get you a good job." Education in general is often geared to practical social action—we go through it to gain "useful skills," to learn how to "do" something, and to increase our earning potential. Yet there are other reasons for education. As Benton & Craib argue, "through education we become better people, more sensitive, able to appreciate the true and the beautiful, able to find sophisticated pleasures in the world; we become better citizens" (p. 78). But why is this type of social action, based more on values than practicality, seemingly less valued in contemporary society? Weber provides us with an important perspective. As society modernizes, the rise of market economies and bureaucratic processes favor more practical, or instrumental, rationality. As Dodd (1999) states (p. 42):

> Weber's account of the Protestant ethic can therefore be read meta-phorically: less as a historical analysis of the emergence of capitalism than as an expression of a much wider transformation of modern society. This consists of the growth of an instrumental worldview in which ultimate values are debased . . . More specifically, he suggests that the expansion of modern industrial capitalism necessarily goes hand in hand with the disenchantment of the world. He characterizes this process as the increasing intellectualization and rationalization of life.

Here we see Weber's normative critique of the process of modernization. The growth of modernity has yielded conditions that favor a particular type of rationality—that of instrumental or means–ends rationality. This process can best be understood as rationalization which, according to Dodd, "does not provide us with a more well rounded understanding of the conditions under which we live. Rather, it mistakenly suggests that we can master everything by rational calculation" (p. 42).

Such hubris, argued Weber, would lead to increasing use of means–ends think-ing, in essence becoming a self-perpetuating system. For example, as moderniza-tion accelerates, organizations grow increasingly more complex and layered. As a result, bureaucratic structures are implemented to "manage" the complexity. In terms of schooling and schools, this can be clearly seen in the rise of the school consolidation movement. Smaller schools are merged into fewer, large schools enabling an efficient centralization of resources. However, as a result, conditions are created that favor instrumental rationality (as evidenced by our current system of testing and assessment, the rise in school administrators, and the overall complexity of the system). As Weber (1930) himself wrote: "For of the last stage of this cultural development, it might well be truly said: 'Specialists without spirit, sensualists without heart; this nullity imagines that it has attained a level of civilization never before achieved'" (p. 182). Critics of Weber often cite the seeming inevitability of this process of rationalization as a fundamental flaw of his theory. The process seems outside the workings of culture. How is one to escape this "iron cage" of disenchantment? What explains the grip instrumental ratio-nality has on social action? Whereas Weber tends to explain instrumental rationality as "an abstract system of logic . . . [others] have suggested . . . [that it is] a system of thought which is embedded in historically and culturally specific systems of power" (Dodd, 1999, p. 51).

Habermas and the Colonization of Reason

While Weber's conceptual framework is helpful in understanding the historical conditions that have given rise to modernization and a particular form of reason and rationality, as I noted above, it leaves several key questions unanswered. As Dodd suggests, critics of Weber claim that his conceptual framework seems to float above the historical and cultural milieu. One of the consequences of this abstract iron cage is its relatively weak incorporation of power and ideology. This leaves one pondering where the freedom exists to imagine how things might be otherwise given the seeming inevitability of rationalization. It is here that the work of critical theory and, in particular, Jürgen Habermas can provide important extensions of Weber's conceptual framework. Whereas Weber constructed a homogeneous and abstract process of rationalization, critical theorists would argue that the process of rationalization is not inherent or a given but rather can be explained by certain cultural, political, and ideological factors. Such a move, in the end, provides opportunities for resistance by constructing a social theory set against these subjective processes.

Habermas viewed Weber's distinction between instrumental and value rationality as one of the most important elements of his work (Dodd, 1999). Like the critical theorists of the early Frankfurt school, Habermas also viewed Weber's analysis of rationalization problematically in the sense that it over-emphasized the importance of instrumental reason in modern society. In attempting to correct this, Habermas sought to incorporate Weber's notion of value rationality into a more vigorous and hopeful normative stance. He does this by distinguishing between what he calls the system and the lifeworld, in essence decoupling reason into two major elements of modern society. To Habermas, each of these elements—both the system and the lifeworld—utilizes a particular mode of reason. As the system world is the realm of economic and administrative organizations, the operating logic within it is instrumental. Whereas the lifeworld, including elements such as education, family life, and the media, is constituted primarily by value rationality or what Habermas refers to as communicative reason. To Habermas, the system world, relying on instrumental rationality, becomes problematic when it expands and encroaches upon the lifeworld and the domain of communicative reason. This process becomes a form of colonization whereby formerly public spaces—spaces distinct and separate from the broadly economic world—come under the sway of means–ends thinking. To Habermas, one of the consequences of modernization is this encroachment of the system world into the lifeworld. Importantly, instrumental rationality is not per se a bad thing. Rather, it becomes a cause for concern when rationality becomes reified in one particular manifestation (instrumental), at the expense of other ways of thinking and being in the world. As Dodd (1999) states: "The system has increasingly invaded, or colonized, the lifeworld, stunting its development and distorting the operation of institutions—such as family and the education system —which reside there" (p. 115). This systemic distortion, to Habermas, can be combated only by cultivating a "hermeneutics of suspicion" and reinvigorating communicative reason (Benton & Craib, 2001). Only through this activity in the public sphere can we discover a more liberatory social action that resists the negative consequences of modernity.

Many have taken issue with Habermas's seeming over-reliance on the "ideal speech situation" and communicative reason to combat the colonization of the lifeworld. Indeed, as Benton & Craib argue, "Habermas can be criticized for an over-rational view of humans and society" (2001, p. 117). My point here is not to cover Habermas's and Weber's extensive and complex social theory in detail, but rather to illustrate a unique historical and theoretical backdrop that helps frame the rise of what I will label as "neo-experientialism" in education. For the remainder of this chapter, we will examine the ways in which this encroachment or colonization has affected the field of experiential education. In what follows, we will first explore the rise of what Engel calls "market ideology" within educational settings and connect this with George Ritzer's (2001) notion of "McDonaldization," to capture how instrumental reason is colonizing public spaces in education. We will then move on to examples of this phenomenon in the field of experiential education, concluding with several key characteristics of this process of "neo-experientialism" and why it should be cause for concern.

Market Ideology and the McDonaldization of Experience

As Habermas argued, the processes of modernization and rationalization favor the interests of capital production and those in positions of economic and cultural power by defining reason in particular ways and for particular purposes. One particular manifestation of this process can be seen in the rise of market ideology in the public space of schooling. As Engel (2000) argues (pp. 3–6):

> Current-day discussions about the future of education are conducted almost entirely in the language of the free market: individual achievement, competition, choice, economic growth, and national security—with only occasional lip service being given to egalitarian and democratic goals . . . market ideology's virtually unchallenged dominance threatens the very existence of public education as a social institution, because its logic ultimately eliminates any justification for collective and democratic control of schools.

Often tied to neo-liberalism,[2] this market ideology has, as Engel argues, come to dominate the discourse on education in the West. How does this market ideology impact schools? There myriad effects have been well documented in the literature (Apple, 2006; Bowles & Gintis, 1976; MacLeod, 1995). Here, I will examine one particular perspective drawing from the work of George Ritzer. Ritzer's concept of the process of McDonaldization aptly draws together a Weberian framework within the discourse of neo-liberalism and market ideology. In addition, the processes he describes overlay well with the defining characteristics of neo-experientialism.

Ritzer (2001) describes the ways in which society as a whole begins to take on the characteristics of the fast-food company, McDonald's. Ritzer defines McDonaldization as (p. 198, emphasis added):

> the process by which the principles of the fast food restaurant are coming to dominate more and more sectors of American society as well as the rest of the world. McDonaldization affects not only the restaurant business but also *education*, work, health care, travel, leisure, dieting, politics, the family and virtually every other aspect of society. McDonaldization has shown every sign of being an inexorable process by sweeping through *seemingly impervious institutions* and parts of the world.

Ritzer goes on to identity four dimensions to McDonaldization: efficiency, calculability, predictability, and control. First, just as the fast-food industry has

---

2 See Hayek (1960), *The Constitution of Liberty*. Hayek is often seen as the "founding father of neoliberalism" (Karaba, 2008) in the way he constructs a particularly individual and self-interested notion of freedom.

organized itself around the minimization of time and extraneous effort and the maximization of productivity, so too have other sectors of society begun to value and adhere to the modes of efficiency. Second, Ritzer argues that calculability—defined as the desire to quantify things and the tendency to rationalize value from quantity rather than quality—is a growing trend. "Quantity has become equivalent to quality; a lot of something, or the quick delivery of it, means it must be good" (Ritzer, 2001, p. 199).

Third, McDonald's emblematizes consistency and predictability through the idea that the product you get from one place to another will be the same. To Ritzer, this goes beyond a guarantee that the Big Mac one eats in New York will be the same as the Big Mac one gets in Los Angeles (or Buenos Aires for that matter). Predictability also permeates into organizational structures and human resources through the concept of scripting. Employees are expected to follow scripts in their interactions with customers in order to ensure consistency with worker–customer interactions. Finally, there is an element of control. Ritzer emphasizes the role of technology in this dimension of McDonaldization: "control, especially through substitution of nonhuman for human technology, is exerted over the people who enter the world of McDonald's" (p. 201). By controlling the amount of human influence on the product, McDonald's is able to control the quality and level of service, thus contributing to a consistent product to the customer. Ritzer is also quick to point out that a critique of McDonald's and the process of McDonaldization does not necessitate a Pollyanna return to a simpler time. His focus is progressive—on the possible consequences of this process for the future. "The future in this sense is defined as human potential, unfettered by the constraints of McDonaldized systems. This critique holds that people have the potential to be far more thoughtful, skillful, creative, and well rounded than they are now" (Ritzer, 2001, p. 203).

Characteristics of Neo-Experiential Education

Neo-experiential education plays itself out in a myriad ways of formal and informal curriculum settings from environmental education experiences, to service learning programs, to more traditional classroom activities. Yet, what are the distinct characteristics of this phenomenon on our river of experience? As we noted at the beginning of this chapter, this particular manifestation of experi-ence in education is not so much of a "current" in the river we have been exploring but rather a phenomenon in the larger "landscape" that impacts the river itself. This is due to the fact that this current is not consciously employed within the field but rather represents a growing influence on the way experience is employed in a host of formal and informal curriculum projects. To return to our thematic metaphor, the "hardscaping" of the land around a river makes it more vulnerable to run-off and "pulses." Water, in essence, runs more "efficiently" through the system, washing out the distinct variations and covering over diverse characteristics as it finds the fastest and least obstructed pathway downstream. In this sense, neo-experientialism increasingly seems to be colonizing the other currents we have discussed by normalizing a particular construction of experience.

Within this worldview, the individual is a rational consumer presented with choices. Experience itself becomes a consumable product, varying little from any other product in the educational marketplace. Neo-experiential frameworks "commodify" experience as an individual choice. As Giroux (1999) argues, "None of us stands outside of the cultures of pleasure and entertainment that now hold such sway over American society" (p. 12). Experience, in this way, is equated with pleasure and entertainment as typified by the increased popularity of "extreme sports" and the "edutainment" of media elements such as Channel One. As Apple (2006) states: "Students, in essence, are sold as captive audience to [Channel One] . . . Thus, under a number of variants of neoliberalism not only are schools transformed into market commodities, but so too now are our children" (p. 42). Matthew Crawford, author of *Shop Class as Soulcraft*, recounts a telling example when he describes "Build-a-Bear"—a currently popular store in shopping malls.

> One of the hottest things at the shopping mall right now is a store called Build-a-Bear, where children are said to make their own teddy bears. I went into one of these stores, and it turns out that what the kid actually does is select the features and clothes for the bear on a computer screen, then the bear is made for him. Some entity has *leaped in* ahead of us and taken care of things already, with a kind of solicitude. The effect is to preempt cultivation of embodied agency, the sort that is natural to us. Children so preempted will be more well adjusted to emerging patterns of work and consumption . . . it will not strike them that anything is amiss.
>
> *2009, p. 69, emphasis in text*

Thus, the individual is not located socially, transformatively, or critically (as in each of the previous currents) but rather *consumptively* as a decontextualized and depoliticized individual consumer. As neo-experientialism continues to colonize other forms of experience in education, children will, as Crawford describes, become so accustomed they will scarcely know what they are missing. Presented with "experiences" and "choices" and "autonomy," they will happily comply, all the while never realizing that such experiences have been carefully planned and selected *for them*. Yes, you can have it "your way," it's just that "your way" and "our way" turn out to be the same thing.

Just as the individual is decontextualized within this framework, so too is knowledge. By tightly bounding and scripting experiential activity, neo-experiential curricular projects conflate knowledge *with* experience. In essence, they become one and the same. Dewey, for example, made a distinction between what he called "primary" and "secondary" experience (Dewey, 1958). In order for experience to become "educative" it must include the elements of interaction and continuity, both of which were made manifest through the acts of social engagement and reflection. For Freire, praxis involved the on-going dialogic process of action and reflection in the world. Within the neo-experiential current, however, the "real world" and the "classroom world" are falsely dichotomized. Experiential activity occurs "outside" normal curricular space and time. As a result, there is no need for "transfer" of knowledge, per se, as the activity itself is sufficient. Even when transfer is expected and applied, it is packaged in the form of ritualized scripts where students perform vacuous reflective exercises divorced from engaged meaning making. Sakofs (2001), for example, used the metaphor of candy to explain how experiential activities can become trivialized in their application (p. 5):

> I was seeing powerful activities used indiscriminately, without thought, resulting in an unintentional outcome of trivializing them through overuse and/or misapplication. In effect, and in a metaphoric sense, making them candy-sweet and desirable, but with no substance or meaning, or robbed of substance or meaning.

In essence, there is no secondary experience within the neo-experiential education framework. Everything is a primary experience, without interaction, continuity, or context.

So, what then are the ethical dimensions of this "normative" current? Because neo-experiential education is not consciously employed within the field, these ethical aims are more of a consequence than a purposeful philosophical stance. Neo-experiential curriculum projects evoke a type of inclusive utilitarianism— the more efficient we can make the experience, the greater the number of students that might be able to benefit. In addition, by constructing a notion of experience that is ostensibly *neutral*, conflicts and political entanglements can be avoided. To allow for more than "fast-food" experiential activity would threaten the dominant mode of instrumental rationality in schools. It would question fundamental assumptions about the nature of knowledge and the purposes of education. We seem to have no time for such philosophical inquiry as we march forward through modernity. But such questioning is essential. As Giroux (1999) argues in regards to what he calls the "Disnification" of society (p. 11):

> Questioning what Disney teaches is part of a much broader inquiry regard-ing what it is parents, children, educators, and others need to know in order to critique and challenge, when necessary, those institutional and cultural forces that have a direct impact on public life. Such inquiry is most impor-tant at a time when corporations hold such an inordinate amount of power in shaping children's culture into a largely commercial endeavor, using their various cultural technologies as teaching machines to commodify and

homogenize all aspects of everyday life—and in this sense posing a potential threat to the real freedoms associated with a substantive democracy.

Whereas the philosophical roots of experiential education could actually be seen as subversive to the dominant mode of schooling in the United States, in its technical application it becomes quite innocuous and functionalist. "Hands-on" learning, "learning by doing," and "building on prior knowledge" are commonly evoked as common-sense pedagogical approaches. Most teacher training textbooks will argue for their use as an effective classroom method. In this current, experience becomes something technical and instrumental. It is tightly bounded (in both time and space), rationally constructed, and efficiently controlled. "Normal" classroom or school activity stops and experiential activity begins for a bounded and specific timeframe. Thus, experience becomes "neo-experiential" as it fits seamlessly with the current market ideology dominating school structure and organization in the United States today.

Neo-Experiential Current in Experiential Education

There is ample evidence that experience in education is undergoing "colonization" through the processes described above. Examples of neo-experientialism in education are legion, in my view. The rise of the use of ropes courses as a form of experiential education is, perhaps, one of the most visible examples of this trend. Ropes courses (increasingly referred to as "Challenge Courses") were first developed by Outward Bound in the 1960s for use in the United States as a way to accomplish some of the same personal and social outcomes of longer wilderness-based experiences. This particular curriculum project involved generating similar scenarios of perceived risk, individual physical challenge, and interactive problem solving, on a smaller time scale and within a much more localized context. The application quickly caught on as experiential educators realized ropes courses allowed for greater numbers (and a greater diversity) of participants to partake in the benefits of experiential education. Since the first courses in the United States in the 1960s, "challenge education" has grown rapidly to well over six thousand courses worldwide and a professional association, the Professional Ropes Course Association, established in 2003 (Neill, 2004).

While there are certainly many positive elements of ropes course programs in terms of educative outcomes, they embody the McDonaldization of experience in many ways. All four of Ritzer's values are present: efficiency, predictability, calculability, and control. Ropes courses allow for an experiential education "experience" in a shorter period of time, thus making the entire process much more efficient. They also allow for more people to participate while also doing more total activities. For example, in my own work as a challenge course manager, I have worked with schools that wished to run over four hundred students through a one-time, three-to-four hour team building program once per year.

Here, again, we see the encroachment of the system world on the lifeworld as schools increasingly demand quick delivery of educational "products" in high quantities. Finally, predictability and control are also evident in ropes course and challenge education experiences as individual programs become increasingly scripted and bounded in both time and space to meet the other demands of efficiency and calculability. For example, Dan Garvey, past president of Prescott College, in a speech entitled "The Future of Adventure Education" given at the 2002 Rocky Mountain Region Conference of the Association of Experiential Education, discussed four areas that he believed are radically changing within the field of experiential education. In one area, "Learning What We Teach," Garvey argues that we are experiencing a problem of "over processing" in modern applications of experiential theory. So many young people have now attended a number of experiential learning programs that they have become programmed in what to expect and how to respond to placate the teachers. The following portion of the speech is so revealing, it is worth quoting at length:

> We may have to change the message we are delivering to our younger participants. I think we've got a generation of kids that has been overly processed. Many young people have attended a number of experiential activities, and they've learned that some instructors will accept any reasonable response when the student is asked to reflect upon the experience. They know what we want them to say. I joke that many of our current participants know there are two things they can say when they reflect on the power of an experience, no matter what the experience is. First, they say that they have learned trust. If they don't get the appropriate approval, they add the word communication. *We have a generation of kids who will give us exactly what they think we want to hear.*
>
> *Garvey, 2002, p. 29, emphasis added*

As challenge courses embody the McDonaldized elements of predictability and control, more and more students experience an educational process that is increasingly scripted in design and delivery. Dewey's "indeterminate situation" morphs into a tightly bounded "experience-reflection" event that controls the educational moment through a form of ritualized and linear activity and behavior. As Garvey states, "we have a generation of kids who will give us exactly what they think we want to hear" (p. 29).

In addition to the phenomenon of the rise in popularity of ropes courses, there are other trends indicative of neo-experiential education. There is increasing evidence, for example, that people in the United States in general, and students in particular, are spending less time in unstructured or semi-structured outdoor activity (Karieva, 2008). While it is true that not all experiential education takes place in the outdoors, as we noted in Chapter 3, the field has significant connections to outdoor education and recreation. Recent research suggests that environmental education centers have experienced a decline in the number of days per visit from school groups (Lien, personal communication, 2007). In higher education, the last ten years have seen a dramatic rise in outdoor orientation programs for incoming first years. Yet, the actual number of field days has declined (Bell et al., 2010). School playgrounds, as another example, are often devoid of trees or any sort of "unkept" nature. It is often a "built environment" of plastic equipment, rubberized mulch (at least it's recycled), and asphalt. Students rarely have a say in how this space is designed. Even recess has come under fire for its lack of instrumental value to "learning" as defined by tightly prescribed learning outcomes (Barth, 2008). Richard Louv, in his popular book *Last Child in the Woods*, argues that today's children in the United States suffer from "nature deficit disorder." Citing the emergence of a "third frontier" that will shape the way the current generation of children perceive nature, Louv (2006) identifies five key trends (p. 19):

> a severance of the public and the private mind from our food's origins; a disappearing line between machines, humans, and other animals; an increased intellectual understanding of our relationship with other animals; the invasion of our cities by wild animals (even as urban/suburban designers replace wildness with synthetic nature); and the rise of a new kind of suburban form.

In significant ways, students' experiential contact with the natural world is being curtailed and shaped under the auspices of "seat time" and "time on task." When they are "allowed" outside, their contact is structured, prescribed, and limited. As the dominant currency of school becomes seat time, the kind of inductive learning that arises from relatively unstructured, outdoor activity is increasingly marginalized. "Loose parts" learning and play, the kind where children, in the words of Dorothy Lee (1986), are asked to be "lost in ambiguity and [then build] a world out of it" (p. 42), are subsumed under the efficiency and calculability of standardization.

There is evidence of neo-experientialism within the more traditional school curriculum as well. With the rise in popularity and use of service learning curriculum, more students experience "service" but it is less clear that they are learning any particular virtues of civichood by completing a mandatory number of community volunteer hours. Concerns have arisen in regards to the lack of theoretical depth in conceptualizing service learning methodologies. Stanton et al. (1999) argue, "there's not a deep discussion on what makes practice good . . . It's been a first level discussion of getting service learning in place, regardless of quality" (p. 217). Seaman & Gass (2004) cite concerns that the institutionalization of service learning may also affect its transformative or more radical potential. As we explored in the previous chapter, this can lead to the trivialization of service and the reproduction of negative stereotypes as in the college sorority girls' exclaiming that the neighborhood where they were helping build a house was "so ghetto!" Other forms of experiential education in traditional schools are also prone to McDonaldization. The 2008 presidential election inspired many schools around the country to hold their own "mock" elections to demonstrate how our democracy works. Yet, one wonders about what is actually learned in such "experiential" activities. Students proceed to "vote" for a candidate ostensibly to "experience" democracy, votes are tallied, and a "winner" is declared. Yet, it is all a mirage. Their vote does not, in fact, count. And afterward, things return to normal. School continues unchanged and unaffected. What if schools designed an election around something of real consequence to the school itself? What if students could *actually* use their voice in their schools? What would it look like to run not a *simulation* but an *actualization*? Thus, as neo-experientialism across the curriculum takes hold, students "have" experiences, but they are increasingly impoverished ones. They are limited, scripted, and, often, constructed for students in prescribed ways. As Bonnett (2004) argues, this worldview "reaches its completion in a highly instrumental or calculative rationality, a rationality whose essential motive is unfettered mastery" (p. 157).

Conclusion

It ought to be clear to the reader, by now, that I see few redeemable qualities to the rise of neo-experientialism in education. Nonetheless, it is worth noting that this sort of constructed experience has yielded distinct pedagogical successes. As I stated earlier in the introduction to this book, I myself entered into this field through my work on challenge education programs and ropes courses some of which could be viewed as neo-experiential in orientation. It is certainly true that the application of experiential techniques can tap into alternative ways of learning and teaching that yield positive results. In a sense, there is nothing wrong whatsoever with experiential education applied in this way in both formal and informal curriculum projects. As a *method*, neo-experiential techniques are likely quite effective. Indeed, there ought to be a whole host of methods available to the teacher in any given curriculum situation. Dewey, it is often forgotten, felt the same way. He was never against lecturing or direct instruction as a pedagogical tool. We ought not to shy away from employing "learning by doing" activities in the classroom, or scheduling a ropes course, any more than we should avoid lecturing for fear of violating some remote educational ideal.

The point here is that we are undergoing a process whereby experience is conflated with activity and increasingly wedded to larger market forces. When we can no longer imagine how things might be otherwise, the colonization is complete. Neo-experientialism frames a particular way of thinking about and enacting experiential projects in the curriculum. While values such as "freedom," "choice," and "autonomy" are lifted up within such a frame, they too often revolve around personal preference and the ethics of consumerism rather than the ethics of democracy. As Crawford (2009) notes (p. 70):

The watchword here is easiness, as opposed to heedfulness. But because the field of options generated by market forces maps a collective consciousness, the consumer's vaunted freedom within it might be understood as a tyranny of the majority that he has internalized. The market ideal of Choice by an autonomous Self seems to act as a kind of narcotic that the displacing of embodied agency go smoothly, or precludes the development of such agency by providing easier satisfactions.

What are the consequences of such a colonization of experience in education? The kind of citizen we produce under the neo-experiential variation is insufficient both specifically for the objectives of the field of experiential education and for the larger goals of a democratic society. Indeed, our very sense of unity and solidarity becomes based upon consumption rather than creation and participation (Molnar & Reaves, 2002). And, to Dewey (1938, pp. 64–65),

> it may be a loss rather than a gain to escape from the control of another person only to find one's conduct dictated by immediate whim and caprice, that is, at the mercy of impulses into whose formation intelligent judgment has not entered. A person whose conduct is controlled in this way has at most the illusion of freedom. Actually he is directed by forces over which he has no command.

Thus, in a general sense, the neo-experiential current becomes part of a larger problem, rather than a potentially powerful and transformational curriculum response. Prepackaged and sweet (like candy), efficiently and predictably managed (like McDonald's), and slickly produced (like Disney), it can give us only the illusion of freedom. This colonization of experience in education is indicative of larger shifts within educational progressivism as a whole. If experiential education practitioners are to address real concerns of inequality, marginalization, hegemony, and injustice, we must learn a new civichood, one that is based upon the ideals of participation, deliberation, community, and responsibility.

7

EXPERIENCE AND DEMOCRACY

The Hopeful Current

My focal interest is in human freedom, in the capacity to surpass the given
and look at things as if they could be otherwise.

Maxine Greene (1988)

Introduction

Is it possible, given the conditions of modernity and the current colonization of
experience in education to imagine, in Maxine Greene's words, "things as if they
could be otherwise"? Can our river of experience have yet one more current—
a hopeful one—that points toward freedom and possibility? I believe that there
is. Perhaps it is a current that is "not yet" in that it exists only in our imagination.
But if freedom means the ability to surpass the given and imagine again, as Greene
reminds us, then even the *possibility* of such a current points to a more hopeful
future. As we draw our exploration to a close, I would like to engage in such an
act of freedom—imagining what experiential education might yet come to be,
despite the obstacles that might prevent such a vision from coming to fruition.
As I mention in Chapter 1, as a pragmatist, I am not inclined to offer a universal,
one-size-fits-all, construction of the "true" experiential education. Nor am I
interested here in some tight and specific formulation of what is needed to retrieve
experiential education out from under hegemonic control. Such a conclusion
would fly in the face of the anti-universalism, anti-instrumentalism, and fallibilism
that form the basis of the pragmatic orientation. Nonetheless, we cannot with-
draw from the choices or the moral consequences that come with knowledge.
Not choosing, in the end, is still a choice. I have argued that I see a clear and
pressing danger involving the impacts of modernity on the way we talk about
(and enact) experience in education today. As Gowin recounts in the foreword

to Greene's *Dialectic of Freedom*, "we live in a historic period in which much of our knowledge is a form of technocratic rationality and much of our direct experience is privatized, consumerist experience" (1988, p. x). Such a historical moment demands a response—a vision for how things might be otherwise. To give such a response, as a Deweyian, and as someone writing from the context of the United States, necessitates some engagement with the notion of democratic living. Cornell West (2000) once commented that:

> Anyone who has the audacity to adopt a democratic vision cannot be optimistic, though I do not conflate optimism with hope. Why? Because democracies are rare in human history, they are fragile, and historically they tend not to last that long . . . And America has been so privileged because there has always been a prophetic slice across race, region, and class, and gender, and sexual orientation, a progressive slice that says we are not going to give up on this fragile democratic project, it is incomplete and unfinished, but we are not going to give up on it, even against the grain of so much human history.

Experiential education, too, is fragile and incomplete. But, as West reminds us, we need not be optimistic to still have hope. Hope that, even in its fragile and incomplete state, our notions of experiential education can yet be stronger, more robust. In this final current, we'll organize things a little differently. First, we'll return to my earlier recollected experiences at summer camp that began this book when I was full of optimism about the power of experiential education. It was here, during one memorable summer, that I met "Alvin." Alvin's story will serve as our guide through this current, revealing the ways in which experiential education is both fragile and incomplete. From this backdrop, we'll consider how the field might be strengthened, not technically, but rather conceptually—as we examine the connections between experiential education and democratic education. The aim here will be to open the field up to possibility, to imagination, again. But to begin, we have to meet Alvin, our teacher for this current.

Alvin's Story

In 1993, I was a team leader for a nationally known summer program in Lake Forest, Illinois. The camp specializes in brain-based, learning-how-to-learn programs for at-risk youth. Its programs are highly experiential and it was through them, as I mentioned in the Foreword to this book, that I got into this field in the first place. The program targeted at-risk youth, though it was predominantly highly privileged at-risk youth, kids from wealthy families who might have gotten into minor trouble either at school or with the law—the kind of kids popularized by the "Brat Camp" reality television show that came out some years ago. In an effort to diversify the camp, several scholarships were awarded to inner-city youth from South Chicago. Alvin was one of the first recipients and was placed in my group. Alvin was a young fifteen and he still had that roly-poly baby fat that made him seem even younger than he actually was. He was loud and out-going and his brashness (not to mention his skin color) stood him out within the camp community. Things were difficult right off the bat for Alvin. No one else looked like him, talked like him, or came from the same background. He portrayed a tough persona and the other kids in my group mostly kept their distance. During one of our first, intensive group sessions, Alvin spoke openly about the drugs he had done and watched others do. So openly, in fact, that some of the other campers in my group snickered and shook their heads, thinking Alvin was just showing off and not being real about his background and his history. I took to Alvin almost immediately. He had that kind of personality that, even when he was being resistant and uncooperative, he was still engaging and alive. I'd take a thousand Alvins over one tired, dispassionate, and cynical kid.

So I knew that things at camp were likely to change for Alvin and they did. The ropes course day was huge for him. The physical learning and trust he established with his group over the course of that day seemed to shift something in him. Slowly, his energy and brashness turned from getting negative attention to positive encouragement and the support of his group. We have all seen this countless times—camp was doing its magic on Alvin. By the end of the program Alvin was transformed. He cried the final night of camp and made sure to get everyone's phone numbers and addresses before his session ended. I remember the hug I got from Alvin the day he left—he was just a kid needing love—such a simple thing. As he hugged me he leaned in to my ear and whispered a private message, one only for me to hear. He said, "you'll always be my favorite teach . . ."

It is this sort of success story that many teachers know and can appreciate: the transformative power of an educational experience and its ability to reach kids in a way that can shift them, despite previous school failures, challenged background, or diagnosed condition. But, Alvin's story does not end there. His story has more to teach. After Alvin left I got back into the busyness of camp and preparing for the next session. Anyone who has worked at camp knows that, while the kids affect you and you love them, they also come and go. And despite the promises of writing and calling and remaining lifelong friends, things fade over time. With a new set of campers came a new set of challenges and kids who needed support and love. While I certainly hadn't forgotten about Alvin I was somewhat surprised, four days into the next session, when the office paged me and said I had a call from Alvin. I went up and picked up the phone. It was Alvin all right—we traded inside jokes and pleasantries but I also detected an edge to his voice. When I asked how he was doing, he opened up. He couldn't find anyone to talk to about his camp experience back at home. He missed the camp and the group and asked if he could come back. I told him it was against camp policy to come on to grounds if you were not a camper in that session. And besides, how was he going to get up here? He said he understood. He told me that he loved me and

I said I did back—but there was a different emotion in his voice than mine. His was the voice of a kid hanging on to a thin thread of a lifeline. Mine was that of a camp counselor just doing my job. A few days later I got a message from the office that Alvin had called again. During some free time I called him back and, with tears in his voice, he said he was in real trouble. He needed to come back. He didn't have any friends and things were rough at home. I told him all the things we were trained to say about taking ownership for your situation and thinking positively about what you can control. But it was clear that it wasn't what he needed. I remember that we ended that phone call awkwardly. As I walked away from the office, Alvin's "favorite teach" began to have his doubts about what camp had really done for him (or to him?).

About a month after the second call from Alvin that ended awkwardly, I got another message from the office. It was Alvin again and he wanted me to call him back. I'd like to think that I simply forgot or that I got too busy with the next session of camp, but I know better. I never called him back. I didn't want to because I knew I didn't have anything else to say—there was nothing in my training, in my background, or in my manual that told me how to deal with the kind of pain and hurt that Alvin was going through.

A Fragile Project

Alvin's story to this point reveals the ways in which the field of experiential education is fragile. It is fragile in the sense that, for a variety of reasons that I have made clear in this project (the shallow theoretical foundation, the lack of critical awareness, the current economic and political zeitgeist), experiential curriculum projects are vulnerable to cooptation, commodification, and hegemonic control. But Alvin's story gives such distant academic terminology a more personal face. Transformation as such is almost always a fragile process. To become something else, to change one's nature, requires a "death" of sorts. But is this transformation always innocent? Is it always for the better? Alvin was changed by his experience at camp but I am left with a haunting sense that this change was an opening up, a wound of sorts, rather than a complete reconstitution. I am reminded of what W. E. B. Du Bois called racial two-ness—the dilemma of existing in-between worlds—part of both but unable to identify exclusively with either. Richard Rodriguez, in his powerful memoir on bilingual education *Hunger of Memory*, describes the dilemma this way (1982, p. 84):

> From the story of the scholarship boy there is no specific pedagogy to glean. There is, however, a much larger lesson. His story makes clear that education is a long, unglamorous, even demeaning process—a nurturing never natural to the person one was before one entered a classroom . . . [the scholarship boy] both wants to go back and yet thinks he has gone beyond his class, feels weighted with knowledge of his own . . . situation.

The fragility of experiential education, to me, is clear. Alvin's story demonstrates it. While we champion its transformative potential, we forget that the field, and the educational processes employed within it, does not exist outside of history. All of the problems, challenges, and struggles of education, that long and unglamorous process that Rodriguez describes, are written into experiential education too. The "one-off" nature of Alvin's experience reveals significant issues with a field that focuses perhaps too much on "programs" and not enough on "process." The underlying issues of culture and power shot through Alvin's "transformational" experience are too often not adequately addressed in the field.

But I also don't accept Rodriguez's pessimism—that education is by definition a demeaning process. The kind of experiential education represented through Alvin's story does not have to only be seen as damaging. There are so many counter–examples—of lives turned around, light bulbs turned on, and self-confidence found. But Alvin's story reminds me of how fragile it all is. I have never forgotten about Alvin though I do not know how things ended up for him. He was not well served by our so-called transformative experiential education. He spent just enough time with us at camp to open up and reveal the vulner-abilities of a young man needing love, and then he was released, fragile, into a world that he no longer knew how to navigate. And for that, I want to write something to him that I have yearned to say for so long . . . I am sorry. I am sorry I did not call you back. I am sorry you were not given more support. I am sorry that our program and your experience failed both you and us. And, every chance that I get, I will think about ways to do better.

An Incomplete Project

Alvin's story reminds us that experiential education is fragile, but perhaps a more hopeful frame would be to see it not just as fragile but as incomplete. In its incom-pleteness, we see possibility—ways we can actively respond and reconstruct. I see two main ways the field is incomplete—it is too shallow in its "roots" and not productive enough in its "fruits." Both of these areas require real work and, doing that work can strengthen the field moving forward. First, the roots of experiential education, its intellectual ancestry as it were, are too shallow. In some ways, the field is like the Romantic Transcendentalist who has spent a little too much time alone in the wilderness and, upon re-entry, seems uneasy, incapable of translating the power of his experience to others, and perhaps would just prefer to return to his isolated world rather than engage with difference. Experiential education needs to get out of the wilderness in a few specific ways. One is by diversifying the intellectual ancestry of experiential education, opening up room for a wider array of voices. Most people think of John Dewey, Kurt Hahn, maybe Paul Petzhodlt, and perhaps, in the more modern context, David Kolb and his experiential learning cycle. This is a fine list. But it is also a list, with respect, of mostly dead, Western, white men. There are others who have written about the role of experience in education that we do not hear from nor do we expose our students to—women such as Patricia Hill Collins, bell hooks, Nel Noddings, Deb Meier, and Dorothy Lee. There are also those who write from first peoples or non-Western orientations that need to be lifted up. These are silenced or subaltern voices that can enrich and expand the ways we think about experiential education. Doing so deepens and expands the roots of the field, strengthening its stance and broadening its base. So long as the field is known exclusively by some specialized curriculum project (such as wilderness trips or service learning) alone, it will remain marginalized. The way out of that exile is by building relationships, coalitions, and connections across disparate strands of educational progressivism. There is work to be done here.

Besides shallow roots, the other area of incompleteness for experiential education is its under-developed fruits. That is to say, what is the purpose of experiential education? What does it bring forth to the world? Experiential education, as a field, seems at times to under-emphasize the moral consequences of knowledge. Many critique the acquisition of knowledge simply for knowledge's sake as the sole purpose of schooling. I would posit that a similar critique could be leveled at experiential education: activity for activity's sake. The important question is: activity to what further use or purpose? Ben Lawhon (2009), the Education Director for the Leave No Trace Center for Outdoor Ethics, recently recounted the following story. A group of students in the Pacific Northwest were taking a Leave No Trace (LNT) course in a wilderness area, learning about proper tactics for human waste removal while traveling over (and recreating on) glaciers. After the lesson, one of the classroom teachers pulled aside the LNT educator and said: "you spend all this time talking about how to pack out your waste on this glacier with these kids but you never talked about the overall status of this glacier, the fact that it is receding due to climate change, and the impact of those changes on the millions of people down there (pointing to the city) who rely on access to this water for their livelihoods. Why don't you guys talk about *that*?" When "experience" becomes an isolated thing to have and consume it loses its potential to teach any more. Kids learning LNT protocols on a glacier, in the end, is not good enough. It is an incomplete education.

How do the curriculum designs make the world a better, more equitable, more sustainable place? Do we note the irony in flying students to wilderness areas, bussing them to remote locations, emitting tons of carbon into the atmosphere, only *then* to teach them to "leave no trace"? Do service learning programs truly ask students to question and critique a society where such profound inequalities exist? And, when we facilitate programs for the disenfranchised, how much say do these culture groups have in the co-creation of the program and curriculum? Experiential education at its strongest, at its most robust, does not just exist within the activity, but it is in the active construction of the learning process itself. The field will remain incomplete so long as students like Alvin have no say, no voice, in what they are experiencing. Not just in-the-moment, but in allowing, as Deb Meier once said, to truly experience the power of their ideas.

The Impeded Stream

The hopeful current in our river does not yield a five-point plan to make experiential education solid and complete. Rather it reminds us that experiential education may forever exist in that place of being both fragile and incomplete— just as Cornell West described the larger democratic project. Proponents should be aware of this fact, ever vigilant, but also full of hope and celebrating the tensions that arise from this place. Alvin's story reminds me that experiential education doesn't always "work." That sometimes we fail. But I also know that I am committed to this field and this work because of students like Alvin. The fact that we don't have all the answers should not be lamented. It should be celebrated. I find Wendell Berry's (1985) wonderful poem *The Real Work* to be my guide in this:

> It may be that when we no longer know what to do
> We have come to our real work
> And that when we no longer know which way to go
> We have come to our real journey.
> The mind that is not baffled is not employed.
> The impeded stream is the one that sings.

Berry writes of our real work that it is only when we are baffled that our mind is truly employed. He speaks of a stream, that only when impeded, truly "sings." Freedom is enacted when confronting obstacles. Our river of experience is only alive in its conflicts, its tensions, and its multiplicity. The impeded stream simply reminds us that there is much yet to do, more to fight for. Democracy (like freedom) is not, in the end, a birthright, something to grasp and own. It is, as Dewey reminds us, a way of life. It is something to enact, day-to-day, in our relations with others. To Dewey, the self, like democracy, is "something in continuous formation through choice of action" (1916, p. 408).

That is why it is also not enough merely to sit back and critique—something that academia has become all too accomplished at doing. Richard Rorty (1998), in *Achieving Our Country*, described this as the "spectatorial Left." Tearing something down may be easier and certainly more enjoyable as a form of psychic release, but it leaves the hard work yet to be done. It is not demolition but construction that we are after. Parker Palmer (2007), a noted writer on the role of teaching, discusses an old Hasidic tale in his book *The Courage to Teach*. He writes (p. 152):

> I once heard this Hasidic tale: "We need a coat with two pockets. In one pocket there is dust, and in the other pocket there is gold. We need a coat

with two pockets to remind us of who we are." Knowing, teaching, and learning under the grace of great things will come from teachers who own such a coat and who wear it to class every day.

It is not enough to blindly praise the real or imagined laurels of experiential education, nor is it productive to simply criticize the ways it doesn't match up with our ideals and values. An exclusive emphasis on one or the other yields either a mindless optimism or a defeatist cynicism. A vital democratic project thrives on neither of these extremes. An Arizona rancher once told me and a group of students learning about Western water issues that "we need to find ways to rediscover the radical center" in problem solving. A place where we can hold these challenges and opportunities in tension with one another without letting either one go. The true test of intelligence, F. Scott Fitzgerald once said, was the ability to hold two opposing ideas in your head and still find the capacity to act. And the strength of pragmatism, to me, is its call to action. How can we build something of importance through a reinvigorated notion of educative experience in our schools? But as Greene (1988) reminds us, "there is, however, no orientation to bringing something into being if there is no awareness of something lacking" (p. 22). We have to see the incompleteness, the fragility, before we can go about working toward something better. This is the essence of democratic practice. The worry, then, is whether or not we can really "see" well enough to engage in this real work.

The Democratic Current

Despite some of his critics who claim otherwise, Dewey recognized this worry. He was quite concerned about the "eclipse of the public" that keeps it from being "articulate" (1954, p. 184). In a famous debate with Walter Lippmann, Dewey agreed with Lippmann's claim in the *Phantom Public* that democracy was not functional so long as we depend on a public that is incapable of participation. To Lippmann (1993, p. 3):

> The private citizen today has come to feel rather like a deaf spectator in the back row, who ought to keep his mind on the mystery off there, but cannot quite manage to keep awake . . . No newspaper reports his environment so that he can grasp it; no school has taught him how to imagine it; his ideals, often, do not fit with it; listening to speeches, uttering opinions and voting do not, he finds, enable him to govern it. He lives in a world he cannot see, does not understand and is unable to direct.

But while Dewey might have agreed with Lippmann's characterization of the public as presently incapable of both understanding and participating meaningfully in democratic life, he vehemently rejected Lippmann's conclusion—leaving democracy and governance to the role of experts. As Kadlec (2007) recounts "How is it, Dewey asks, that citizens are supposed to be able to perform even the most limited tasks delineated by Lippmann without some baseline level of involvement, knowledge, and organization which Lippmann deems off-limits?" (p. 94). Dewey understood the obstacles present to democratic engagement and participation but, unlike Lippmann's, his conclusion was not to further eclipse the public through specialists and experts but to endeavor to create the conditions necessary for *more* participation, relationship, and freedom. To Dewey (1981), freedom involves "that secure release and fulfillment of personal potentialities which take place only in rich and manifold associations with others" (p. 2).

So, while the notions of experience in education are both fragile and incomplete, we can yet imagine if things were otherwise. Dewey's answer to this fragility and incompleteness was to seek to create the conditions for democratic flourishing rather than, as Lippmann argues, ceding the care of democratic life to philosopher kings. We certainly need fewer distant, educational technocrats with their universal curriculum designs and content standards and more on-the-ground experiential educators, for example. When did the teacher in the classroom become a "curriculum delivery device" instead of a facilitator, an orchestrator, of meaningful experiences for the students in their care? I think Dewey was correct in claiming that the conditions for democratic living begin in social interaction and, in particular, become learned and acted upon in the classroom. It is the indeterminate situation that produces the conditions for freedom and human flourishing. Maxine Greene wrote that "an education for freedom must move beyond function, beyond the subordination of persons to external ends. It must move beyond mere performance to action, which entails the taking of initiatives" (1988, pp. 132–133). We live out our freedom in the process of engaging in the mystery, in the problem, in the indeterminate situation both as teachers and students. Importantly, this is not an individual act. It is an act done "in concert." Hannah Arendt described power as the ability "to act in concert. Power is never the property of an individual; it belongs to a group and remains in existence only so long as the group keeps together" (1972, p. 143). We lose this ability to flourish together, in democratic life, when actions (and experience) become mere performance. When the situation presented is not, in fact, indeterminate, but rather quite determined, even if we may pretend it is otherwise. This is the ultimate definition of a shallow performance—actions in which the script has already been written, the options accounted for. This is not the place of democracy and freedom. It is unreflective and, in the end, controllable and controlling. To defend against this sort of mindless performativity, we need to employ a construction of experience in education that reclaims a deeper form of play.

Progressives have called this form of educational interaction various things throughout the years. But central to all of these, to me, is a certain construction of experience in education. It is a grounded in what Rilke called living the questions themselves. Dorothy Lee (1986) described it this way (p. 86):

In our society our job is to destroy mystery. Mystery is a challenge to solution; I feel uncomfortable until I explain it away. This is why I have to understand—so that I can grasp, so that I am in a position to manipulate. We leave it to our artists and poets to reach the mystery in immediacy, and leave it whole. Cesaire says that Africans "wed" themselves to the mystery. That is what I want to do—to wed myself to inviolate being, to greet and respond.

This, to me, is why Dewey argued so forcefully for the connections between democracy, education, and experience. Experience is the binding agent that weaves democratic education together and keeps it strong. That we have a situation where "experiential education" has come to be a euphemism for "learning by doing" merely reveals how impoverished our notion of democratic schooling has become. At its most robust, experiential education has the potential to become something much, much more. It has the ability to link disparate strands of progressivism and build a new vision of education—one that takes seriously the interactive role of the student, the teacher, and the community in the democratic process.

There is so much allied against this construction of interaction and experience in United States classrooms today. But, as West reminds us, it is too important a construction of education and democratic living to give up on. Experiential education cannot, should not, retreat into exile as a marginalized, "quirky," approach that is the sole domain of a few. Nor should it be watered down into a vacuous learning-by-doing technique used indiscriminately and universally in classrooms. Dewey saw democratic living in "something that comes to be, in a certain kind of growth, in consequences rather than antecedents . . . [we are free] not because of what we statically are, but in so far as we are becoming different from what we have been" (quoted in Greene, 1988, p. 3). In imagining a democratic current in our river, we can see experiential education "becoming different from what we have been." It is in this sense of becoming, of freedom, of mystery, that I choose to imagine (and act on) how things might be otherwise in experiential education.

Conclusion

Thus, if the previous chapter filled our heads with pessimism about the ways in which experience is impoverished and colonized, this chapter is meant to counter that sense. Not with a Pollyanna sensibility that everything will be all right, but in a sense, as Dennis Carlson (2002) once wrote, of having "hope without illusion." I included the story of Alvin here because there is no Hollywood ending—no clear sense of redemption or reconciliation. Sometimes things do fall apart. To deny this would be to deny the difficulties of enacting democratic projects. Yet the hope of the democratic current is in the freedom of the response.

For every hegemonic process there is the potential for counter-hegemonic action. It is not as neat and clean as traveling back in time to change what happened to Alvin or, perhaps, to see him on the street someday and realize that things turned out OK as a Hollywood script would demand. Democratic work is messier than that. What I can do is live with the weight of it and aim to do better. Aim to imagine things otherwise. As I wade out into the river, through the various currents, I can see it there. Tucked up against the far shore. A thin, strong current running fresh and clear. With care, I may yet get there. The hope of that carries me.

AFTERWORD

Ko te awa ko au (I am the river and the river is me)

Maori saying

What, then, is there left to say about experience in education? This project has sought to explore and unravel the taken-for-granted notion of experience in education by suggesting the existence of at least four major theoretical currents, or variations, of experience employed in a variety of curricular projects. Through discussing Romantic, pragmatist, critical, and finally neo-experiential notions of experience in education we have seen the ways in which our rather same-looking river of experience is alive with a host of currents and counter-currents that lead us in different ways and with often opposing aims. Indeed, the more one wades into the concept of experience, the more potentially muddled one can become. While it has not been my intention to arrive at the one true notion of experience here, I certainly had hoped for some semblance of thematic and argumentative coherence and not simply a cacophony of voices. There is, of course, also a danger in any attempt to organize such a slippery term at all. As I mentioned in the Introduction, investigations into the philosophy of experience have often left the investigator hopelessly lost in a theoretical morass (the reader will have to decide whether or not I have avoided a similar fate here). "Experience," as we have seen, is a term chock full of meanings, associations, and orientations. As Peter Fenves argues, "[e]xperience, freedom—these two words are perhaps the most potent slogans in the English language. Anglo-American thought has never ceased to draw on them in order to define its grounds, methods, and goals" (quoted in Jay, 2005, p. 2). It is clear that this river is an important one, both within the fields of education and educational theory as well as in the larger context of social theory and philosophy. Thus, while wading into this river may have been treacherous, it is a project worth doing in the end because the word itself is so vital. And yet, as we have seen here, we have an entire "field"—that of experiential education—that uses the term almost automatically and without sufficient interrogation.

Of course, it would be important to note some of the shortcomings of this particular project as well. It is simply not possible, nor wise I think, to aim for a "complete" theoretically mapping of experience in education. I have left out important currents here, most notably post-structural investigations on experience, as they are simply not evoked within the discourses on experiential education currently. There is good and important work that ought to be done in this area moving forward. But that is another project for another time. There are likely many other ways one might organize the theoretical landscape and a renewed call for such work ought to be encouraged. In recent history, the bulk of "research" in the name of experiential education has focused almost exclusively on relatively shallow "advocacy" studies. Such efforts amounted to a "preaching to the choir" form of advocacy rather than a sustained and deep research agenda. In response to this, and in large part due to the growing post-"No Child Left Behind" political environment that privileges "evidence-based" practice, the fastest growing body of research appears to be empirical and quantitative in orientation.[1] While it is not the way I have chosen to engage the topic at hand, such moves in experiential education ought to be encouraged. I do remain concerned, however, that the current public and political discourse around what counts for "research" in education combined with the disparagement of the (admittedly shallow) history of scholarly work in the field will eclipse the importance of theoretical and philosophical explorations moving forward. Rather than pit "positivist" methodologies against more conceptual work like this one, however, it seems a better (and more Deweyan response) to encourage a both/and rather than an either/or research agenda. It is my hope that, in some small way, this project aims to lend some theoretical and conceptual depth to the research agenda in experiential education. Such work, in conjunction with other, more empirical work, can strengthen the field and better position it to be a more active player in the discourse on curricular and school reform.

We have explored a variety of theoretical currents in our metaphoric river. Some have been stronger, in terms of their usage within experiential education, and some have been weaker, or have run counter to the main currents. I have worked hard, here, at drawing the distinctions between the currents in order to tease apart the taken-for-grantedness of the term as it is currently used in the field. Yet, each of the currents still exists within a singular river. Is there anything that can be said about the river itself? Anything we might tentatively suggest as common, resonant themes, or points of intersection and overlap between

---

1   The recent establishment of SEER (Symposium on Experiential Education Research) and CORE (Council on Research and Evaluation) is indicative of this growing trend.

the various currents? As Hans-Georg Gadamer (Gadamer & Dutt, 2001) noted (pp. 52–53):

> Being experienced does not mean that one now knows something once and for all and becomes rigid in this knowledge; rather, one becomes more open to new experiences. A person who is experienced is undogmatic. Experience has the effect of freeing one to be open to new experience . . . In our experience we bring nothing to a close; we are constantly learning new things.

Heeding Gadamer's suggestion that we "bring nothing to a close," we'll examine several resonant themes in our river that deserve further thinking and inquiry, in the hopes that such a map encourages new explorations and new ways forward in our attempts to make sense and meaning from such a tricky concept.

Commonalities of Experience

One resonant theme in our river is the interplay between experience and otherness. Each of our currents suggests that experience has something to do with an encounter with something new. From Dewey's notion of the indeterminate situation to more Romantic constructions of the sublime or strange experience, there exists some notion that experience—both *Erlebnis* and *Erfahrung*—necessitates an engagement with something more than mere self. Reflecting back to the chapter on etymology, experience has root meanings in "expereri," meaning to try but also "periculum," meaning danger (Jay, 2005). Thus, in some sense, thinking about experience in education means considering the ways in which notions such as "risk" and "challenge" are embedded in the act of having an educative "experience." As Jay states (p. 403):

> For if we take seriously the notion that experience in virtually all of its guises involves at least a potential learning process produced by an encounter with something new, an obstacle or a challenge that moves the subject beyond where it began, then the necessity of an outside to the interiority of the subject is hard to deny.

An aphorism attributed to Kurt Hahn states, "a ship is safe in the harbor; but that is not what ships are made for." Thus, experience as evoked in experiential education, suggests some commonality around the notions of risk, challenge, and encounters with newness. Dewey (1958) once wrote that experience was "a call to effort, a challenge to investigation, a potential of disaster and death" (pp. 49–50). Experience, taken seriously, suggests the possibility of something far greater than a possession, an ephemeral state, or a disembodied memory. Rilke, the wonderful German poet, once wrote, "surely all art is the result of one's having been in danger, of having gone through an experience all the way to the end, where no one can go any further. The further one goes the more private, the more personal, the more singular an experience becomes, and the thing one is making is, finally the necessary, the irrepressible" (quoted in *Orion*, November–December, 2009, p. 20). This is powerful, subversive stuff. Placing experience at the center of the curriculum endeavor is certainly no Pollyanna-like guarantee of educational success. But its promise lies in its potential and in the possibility of what may be reconstructed moment to moment. It is this potential that attracts so many to the shores of experiential education. Taken seriously, to its fullest potential, experiential education has important things to say about freedom, democracy, and the faith in human potential.

Yet, significantly, experience-as-danger also suggests some peril in how we frame the Other in experiential education. As we have seen within the Romantic variation of experience, the notion of the sublime in relation to Nature set in motion a dichotomizing of the human and natural worlds that the environmental movement continues to struggle with today. In addition, the historic homogeneity of the field suggests that, while there may be the *potential* for new encounters, experience can seemingly become normalized and impoverished such that the Other does not become fully engaged and transacted with in any meaningful way.

This brings us to a second resonant theme. While not all the currents discussed in this project held this particular notion, a variety of voices worried aloud about the diminishment of experience in the modern world. Romantics like Thoreau, progressives such as Dewey, and critical theorists like Adorno all felt that experience had the potential to lose its vitality given the social conditions of modernity. To Jay (2005, p. 407):

> When our society is called an *Erlebnisgesellschaft* [experience-driven] by sociologists who point to the commodification of experiences as one of the most prevalent tendencies of our age, ranging from extreme sports to packaged tourism, they are not celebrating that development. What one might, in fact, say is that the very notion of experience as a commodity is precisely the opposite of what . . . an experience should be, that is, something which can never be fully possessed by its owner.

If much of the way we view experience in society today is *Erlebnisgesellschaft*, how can we respond otherwise as educators? As citizens? Here again there are no easy answers, no ready-made curriculum plans. It requires us to use our imaginations again. To rekindle the power of experience in education and resist the siren-call of commodification, of satisfaction, and ease. As a teaching colleague of mine once remarked, "we need to be comfortable with being uncomfortable" again.

Heraclitus famously said that one never steps into the same river twice. At the conclusion of this project, I certainly feel that way. The metaphor of the river of experience that helped frame this project has already changed. It has changed as the result of the *experience* of writing. Rather than think of these written pages as a statement on something, which seems to me to imply something static and fixed, I would like to yield to a final resonant theme from our currents: that experience, if it is anything, involves a creative bringing forth into the world. Indeed the root "ex" means a bringing forth from (Jay 2005). Many of the currents explored here viewed experience in this way—as an opening up to the world. Thus, rather than a funnel beginning with something wide and closing in, I view this project the opposite way, beginning with the narrow (that of a taken-for-granted notion of experience in experiential education) and, through the exploration of a variety of theoretical currents, a progressive widening out. To extend our river metaphor, the river, in the end, winds down to the sea. There, the lines between river and sea blend and interpenetrate. There is no before and after; no dividing line; no stopping point. What does remains constant is the horizon line, suggesting a way forward, with many choices, but no final destination. And yet, because of this journey, I will never think about experience the same way again. The encounter has left me changed. And the river flows on.

REFERENCES

Abram, D. (1997). *The Spell of the Sensuous: Perception and Language in a More-than-Human World*. New York: Vintage Books.

Adams, D. (1997). *Education for Extinction: American Indians & the Boarding-School Experience, 1875–1928*. Lawrence: University Press of Kansas.

Adkins, C., & Simmons, B. (2002). *Outdoor, Experiential, and Environmental Education: Converging or Diverging Approaches?* ERIC Clearinghouse on Rural Education and Small Schools, AEL, *ERIC Digest, EDO-RC-02-1*.

Apple, M. W. (2004). *Ideology and Curriculum*. New York: Routledge.

Apple, M. W. (2006). *Educating the "Right" Way: Markets, Standards, God, and Inequality*, second edition. New York: Routledge.

Arendt, H. (1958). *The Human Condition*. Chicago: University of Chicago Press.

Arendt, H. (1972). *Crisis of the Republic*. New York: Harcourt Brace Jovanovich.

Association for Experiential Education (2008). Retrieved July 31, 2008, from http://www.aee.org.

Barks, C. (1995). *The Essential Rumi*. New York: HarperCollins.

Barnhardt, R. (2008). "Indigenous Knowledge Systems and Alaska Native Ways of Knowing." *Anthropology & Education Quarterly, 36*(1), 8–23.

Barth, P. (2008). "Time Out: Is Recess in Danger?" The Center for Public Education. Retrieved December 12, 2008, from http://www.centerforpubliceducation.org/.

Basso, K. (1996). *Wisdom Sits in Places: Landscape & Language Among Western Apache*. Santa Fé: University of New Mexico Press.

Beane, J. A. (1997). *Curriculum Integration*. New York: Teachers College Press.

Bell, B., Holmes, M., & Williams, B. (2010). "A Census of Outdoor Orientation Programs at Four-Year Colleges in the United States." *Journal of Experiential Education, 33*(1), 1–18.

Bell, M. (1993). "What Constitutes Experience? Rethinking Theoretical Assumptions." *Journal of Experiential Education, 16*(1), 19–24.

Benton, T., & Craib, I. (2001). *Philosophy of Social Science: The Philosophical Foundations of Social Thought*. New York: Palgrave.

Berlin, I. (1999). *The Roots of Romanticism*. Princeton: Princeton University Press.

Bernstein, R. J. (1992). *The New Constellation*. Cambridge, MA: MIT Press.

Berry, W. (1985). *Collected Poems, 1957–1982*. San Francisco: North Point Press.

Biesta, G., & Burbules, N. C. (2003). *Pragmatism and Educational Research*. Oxford: Rowman & Littlefield Publishers.

Bonnett, M. (2004). *Retrieving Nature: Education for a Post-Humanist Age*. Malden, MA: Wiley-Blackwell.

Bowers, C. A. (1997). *The Culture of Denial: Why the Environmental Movement Needs a Strategy for Reforming Universities and Public Schools*. Albany: State University of New York Press.

Bowers, C. A. (2003). "The Case against John Dewey as an Environmental and Eco-Justice Philosopher." *Environmental Ethics*, *25*(1), 25–42.

Bowles, S., & Gintis, H. (1976). *Schooling in Capitalist America: Educational Reform and the Contradictions of Economic Life*. New York: Basic Books.

Bransford, J. (2000). *How People Learn: Brain, Mind, Experience, and School*. Washington, DC: National Academies Press.

Breunig, M. (2005). "Turning Experiential Education and Critical Pedagogy Theory into Praxis." *Journal of Experiential Education*, *28*(2), 17–32.

Breunig, M. (2008). "Turning Experiential Education & Critical Pedagogy Theory into Praxis." In K. Warren, D. Mitten, & T.A. Loeffler (eds), *The Theory and Practice of Experiential Education*, (pp. 469–483). Boulder: Association for Experiential Education.

Brooks, J. G., & Brooks, M. G. (1999). *In Search of Understanding—The Case for Constructivist Classrooms*, revised edition. Alexandria, VA: Association for Supervision and Curriculum Development.

Caine, R. N., & Caine, G. (1991). *Making Connections: Teaching and the Human Brain*. Alexandria, VA: Association for Supervision and Curriculum Development.

Callicott, J. B. (1998). "The Wilderness Idea Revisited." In J. B. Callicott & M. P. Nelson (eds.), *The Great New Wilderness Debate*. Athens: University of Georgia Press.

Capra, F. (1997). *The Web of Life: A New Synthesis of Mind and Matter*. London: Flamingo Press.

Carlson, D. (2002). *Leaving Safe Harbors: Toward a New Progressivism in American Education and Public Life*. New York: Routledge.

Collins, P. H. (2000). *Black Feminist Thought: Knowledge, Consciousness, and the Politics of Empowerment*. New York: Routledge.

Crawford, M. B. (2009). *Shop Class as Soulcraft: An Inquiry into the Value of Work*. London: Penguin Press.

Cronon, W. (1996). *Uncommon Ground: Rethinking the Human Place in Nature*. New York: W. W. Norton & Company.

Crosby, A. (1981). "A Critical Look: The Philosophical Foundations of Experiential Education." *Journal of Experiential Education*, *4*(1), 9–15.

Dean, B. (2007). "American Wilderness: A New History." In M. L. Lewis (ed.), *Natural History, Romanticism, and Thoreau* (pp. 73–89). Oxford: Oxford University Press.

Delpit, L. (1995). *Other People's Children: Cultural Conflict in the Classroom*. New York: The New Press.

Denevan, W. (1998). "The Pristine Myth: The Landscape of the Americas in 1492." In J. B. Callicott & M. P. Nelson (eds.), *The Great New Wilderness Debate* (pp. 414–442). Athens: University of Georgia Press.

Dewey, J. (1916). *Education and Democracy*. New York: Macmillan.

Dewey, J. (1927/1954). *The Public and Its Problems*. Athens, OH: Swallow Press.

Dewey, J. (1934). *Art as Experience.* New York: G. P. Putnam's Sons.

Dewey, J. (1938). *Experience and Education.* New York: Collier Macmillan.

Dewey, J. (1958). *Experience and Nature.* New York: Courier Dover Publications.

Dewey, J. (1981). *The Later Works, 1925–1953.* Carbondale: Southern Illinois University Press.

Diggins, J. P. (1994). *The Promise of Pragmatism.* Chicago: University of Chicago Press.

Dodd, N. (1999). *Social Theory and Modernity.* Malden, MA: Polity Press.

Eastman, C. ([1916] 1977). *From the Deep Woods to Civilization.* Lincoln: University of Nebraska Press.

Eastman, C. A. (1902). *Indian Boyhood.* New York: Dover.

Ellsworth, E. (1989). "Why Doesn't This Feel Empowering? Working through the Repressive Myths of Critical Pedagogy." *Harvard Educational Review, 59*(3), 297–324.

Engel, M. (2000). *The Struggle for Control of Public Education: Market Ideology vs. Democratic Values.* Philadelphia, PA: Temple University Press.

Fenwick, T. J. (2001). *Experiential Learning: A Theoretical Critique from Five Perspectives.* Columbus, OH: ERIC Clearinghouse on Adult, Career, and Vocational Education.

Foreman, D. (1998). "Wilderness Areas for Real." In J. B. Callicott & M. P. Nelson (eds.), *The Great New Wilderness Debate* (pp. 395–407). Athens: University of Georgia Press.

Fox, K. (2008). "Rethinking Experience: What Do We Mean by this Word 'Experience'?" *Experiential Education, 31*(1), 37–54.

Frankl, V. (1985). *Man's Search for Meaning,* New York: Washington Square Press.

Freire, P. (1970). *Pedagogy of the Oppressed.* New York: Continuum.

Fried, R. L. (2001). *Passionate Teacher.* Boston: Beacon.

Fuss, D. (1989). *Essentially Speaking: Feminism, Nature & Difference.* New York: Routledge.

Gadamer, H. G., & Dutt, C. (2001). *Gadamer in Conversation: Reflections and Commentary.* New Haven: Yale University Press.

Garber, D. (1998). "Descartes, or the Cultivation of the Intellect." In *Philosophers on Education: New Historical Perspectives* (pp. 124–138). London: Routledge.

Gardner, H. (1993). *Frames of Mind: The Theory of Multiple Intelligences.* New York: Basic Books.

Garrison, J., & Neiman, A. (2003). "Pragmatism and Education." In N. Blake, P. Smeyers, R. Smith, & P. Standish (eds.), *The Blackwell Guide to the Philosophy of Education* (pp. 21–37). Malden, MA: Blackwell Publishers.

Garvey, D. (2002). "The Future Role of Experiential Education in Higher Education." *Zip Lines: The Voice for Adventure Education, 44,* 22–25.

Giroux, H. A. (1999). *The Mouse that Roared: Disney and the End of Innocence.* New York: Rowman & Littlefield Publishers.

Gowin, D. B. (1988). "Foreword." In M. Greene, *The Dialectic of Freedom* (pp. ix–x). New York: Teachers College.

Greene, M. (1988). *The Dialectic of Freedom.* New York: Teachers College.

Greene, M., & Griffiths, M. (2003). "Feminism, Philosophy and Education: Imagining Public Spaces." In N. Blake, P. Smeyers, R. Smith, & P. Standish (eds.), *The Blackwell Guide to the Philosophy of Education* (pp. 73–92). Malden, MA: Wiley-Blackwell.

Gruenewald, D. A. (2003). "Foundations of Place: A Multidisciplinary Framework for Place-Conscious Education." *American Educational Research Journal, 40*(3), 619–654.

Guha, R. (1998). "Radical American Environmentalism and 'Wilderness' Preservation: A Third World Critique." In J. B. Callicott & M. P. Nelson (eds.), *The Great New Wilderness Debate.* Athens: University of Georgia Press.

Hames, R. (2007). "The Ecologically Noble Savage Debate." *Annual Review of Anthropology, 36*, 177–190.

Hawken, P. (2007). *Blessed Unrest: How the Largest Social Movement in History Is Restoring Grace, Justice, and Beauty to the World.* New York: Penguin.

Hay, P. R. (2002). *Main Currents in Western Environmental Thought.* Bloomington: Indiana University Press.

Hayek, F. A. (1960). *The Constitution of Liberty.* Chicago: University of Chicago Press.

Hess, S. (2010). "Imagining an Everyday Nature." *Interdisciplinary Studies in Literature, 17*, 85–112.

Hewitt, R. (2002). "Democracy and Power: A Reply to John Dewey's Leftist Critics." *Education and Culture, 19*(2), 1–13.

Hirsch, E. D. (1996). *The Schools We Need and Why We Don't Have Them.* New York: Doubleday Books.

Holman, D., Pavlica, K., & Thorpe, R. (1997). "Rethinking Kolb's Theory of Experiential Learning in Management Education: The Contribution of Social Constructionism and Activity Theory." *Management Learning, 28*(2), 135.

hooks, b. (1994). *Teaching to Transgress: Education as the Practice of Freedom.* New York: Routledge.

Horkheimer, M. (1976). "Traditional and Critical Theory." In P. Connerton (ed.), *Critical Sociology: Selected Readings* (p. 213). New York: Penguin.

Houser, N., & Klousel, C. J. W. (1992). *The Essential Peirce: Selected Philosophical Writings. Vol. 1, (1867–1893).* Bloomington: Indiana University Press.

Hunt, J. (1995). "Dewey's Philosophical Method and Its Influence on His Philosophy of Education." In K. Warren, D. Mitten, & T. A. Loeffler (eds.), *The Theory and Practice of Experiential Education* (pp. 203–212). Boulder: Association for Experiential Education.

Hyde, M. (2008). Keynote Address at the International Association for Experiential Education conference, Vancouver, WA. November 7, 2008.

Illich, I. (1990). "To Hell with Good Intentions." In J. Kendall (ed.), *Combining Service and Learning: A Resource Book for Community and Public Service, 1* (pp. 314–320). Mount Royal, NJ: National Society for Internships and Experiential Learning.

Itin, C. M. (1999). "Reasserting the Philosophy of Experiential Education as a Vehicle for Change in the 21st Century." *Journal of Experiential Education, 22*(2), 91–98.

James, T. (2000). "Can the Mountains Speak for Themselves?" *Scisco Conscientia, 3*, 1–4.

James, T. (2008). "Sketch of a Moving Spirit." In K. Warren, D. Mitten, & T. A. Loeffler (eds.), *The Theory and Practice of Experiential Education* (pp. 105–115). Boulder: Association for Experiential Education.

James, W. (1907). *Pragmatism, a New Name for Some Old Ways of Thinking: Popular Lectures on Philosophy.* New York: Longmans, Green.

Jarvis, K. (2007). "Gender and Wilderness Conservation." In M. L. Lewis (ed.), *American Wilderness: A New History.* Oxford: Oxford University Press.

Jaus, H. R. (1982). *Aesthetic Experience and Literature Hermeneutics.* Minneapolis: University of Minnesota Press.

Jay, M. (2005). *Songs of Experience: Modern American and European Variations on a Universal Theme.* Berkeley: University of California Press.

Jefferson, T. (1944). *The Life and Selected Writings of Thomas Jefferson.* New York: Modern Library.

Kadlec, A. (2007). *Dewey's Critical Pragmatism.* Lanham, MD: Lexington Books.

Karaba, R. (2008). *Making Sense of Freedom in Education: Three Elements of Neoliberal and*

Pragmatic Philosophical Frameworks. Unpublished doctoral dissertation, Miami University, Oxford, OH.

Karieva, P. (2008). "Ominous Trends in Nature Recreation." *Proceedings of the National Academy of Science, 105*(8), 2757–2758.

Kilpatrick, W. H. (1951). *The Education of Man—Aphorisms*. New York: Philosophical Library.

Knapp, C. (2001). *Lasting Lessons: A Teacher's Guide to Reflecting on Experience*. Charleston, WV: ERIC Press.

Kraft, R. J. (1995). "Closed Classrooms, High Mountains and Strange Lands: An Inquiry into Culture and Caring." In K. Warren, D. Mitten, & T. A. Loeffler (eds.). (1995), *The Theory and Practice of Experiential Education* (pp. 8–15). Boulder: Association for Experiential Education.

LaDuke, W. (1999). *All Our Relations*. Cambridge, MA: South End Press.

Lawhon, Ben (2009). Keynote Address to the Midwest Regional Association for Experiential Education. March 28, George Williams College, Wisconsin.

Lee, D. (1986). *Valuing the Self: What We Can Learn from Other Cultures*. Prospect Heights, IL: Waveland Press.

Lippmann, W. (1993). *The Phantom Public*. Piscataway, NJ: Transaction Press.

Lloyd, G. (1991). *Methods and Problems in Greek Science*. Cambridge: Cambridge University Press.

Louv, R. (2006). *Last Child in the Woods: Saving Our Children from Nature-Deficit Disorder*. Chapel Hill, NC: Algonquin Books.

Macedo, D. (2000). "Introduction to the Anniversary Edition." In P. Freire (ed.), *Pedagogy of the Oppressed* (pp. 11–28). New York: Continuum.

MacLeod, J. (1995). *Ain't No Makin' It: Aspirations and Attainment in a Low-Income Neighborhood*. Boulder, CO: Westview Press.

McDermott, R. (1987). "Achieving School Failure: An Anthropological Approach to Illiteracy and Social Stratification." In G. Spinder (ed.), *Education and Cultural Process: Anthropological Approaches* (pp. 173–209). Long Grove, IL: Waveland Press.

McIntosh, P. (1989, July/August). "White Privilege: Unpacking the invisible backpack." *Peace and Freedom*, 49, 10–12.

McLaren, P. (1998). *Life in Schools. An Introduction to Critical Pedagogy in the Foundations of Education*. Reading, MA: Addison Wesley Longman, Inc.

Mead, G. H. (1934). *Mind, Self & Society from the Standpoint of a Social Behaviorist [by] George H. Mead, Edited, with Introduction, by Charles W. Morris*. Chicago: The University of Chicago Press.

Meier, D. (1995). *The Power of Their Ideas*. Boston: Beacon Press.

Merchant, C. (1989). *Ecological Revolutions: Nature, Gender, and Science in New England*. Chapel Hill: The University of North Carolina Press.

Michelson, E. (1996). "Usual Suspects: Experience, Reflection and the (en) Gendering of Knowledge." *International Journal of Lifelong Education, 15*(6), 438–454.

Molnar, A., & Reaves, J. A. (2002). "The Growth of Schoolhouse Commercialism and the Assault on Educative Experience." *Journal of Curriculum and Supervision, 18*(1), 17–55.

Nabhan, G. P. (1997). *Cultures of Habitat*. Washington, DC: Counterpoint Press.

Nabhan, G. P. (2003). *Singing the Turtles to Sea: The Comcáac (Seri) Art and Science of Reptiles*. Berkeley: University of California Press.

Nash, R. (1982). *Wilderness and the American Mind*. New Haven: Yale University Press.

Neill, J. (2004). "History of Ropes Courses." Retrieved November 17, 2008, from: http://wilderdom.com/ropes/RopesHistory.html.

Noddings, N. (2006). *Philosophy of Education*. Boulder: Westview Press.

Nold, J. J. (1977). "On Defining Experiential Education: John Dewey Revisited." *Voyageur*, 1.

Nold, J. (1995). "The Theory and Practice of Experiential Education." In K. Warren, D. Mitten, & T. A. Loeffler (eds.), *The Theory and Practice of Experiential Education*. Boulder: Association for Experiential Education.

Oakeshott, M. (1933). *Experience and Its Modes*. Cambridge: Cambridge University Press.

Orr, D. W. (2002). *The Nature of Design: Ecology, Culture, and Human Intention*. Oxford: Oxford University Press.

Palmer, P. J. (2007). *The Courage to Teach: Exploring the Inner Landscape of a Teacher's Life*. San Francisco: Jossey-Bass.

Parajuli, P. (2001). "Do Four Trees Make a Jungle?" In D. Rothenberg & M. Ulvaeus (eds.), *The World and the Wild*. (pp. 3–20). Tucson: University of Arizona Press.

Priest, S., & Miles, J. C. (1990). *Adventure Education*. State College, PA: Venture Publications.

Proudman, B. (1995). "What Is Experiential Education?" In K. Warren, D. Mitten, & T. A. Loeffler (eds.), *The Theory and Practice of Experiential Education* (pp. 235–248). Boulder: Association for Experiential Education.

Reynolds, M. (1999). "Critical Reflection and Management Education: Rehabilitating Less Hierarchical Approaches." *Journal of Management Education*, *23*(5), 537.

Rilke, M. R. (1986). *Rodin and Other Prose Pieces*. London: Quartet Books.

Ritzer, G. (2001). *Explorations in Social Theory: From Metatheorizing to Rationalization*. Thousand Oaks, CA: Sage Publications.

Roberts, J. (2005). "Disney, Dewey, and the Death of Experience in Education." *Education and Culture*, *21*(2), 12–30.

Roberts, J. (2008). "From Experience to Neo-Experientialism: Variations on a Theme." *Experiential Education*, *31*(1), 19–35.

Rodriguez, R. (1982). *Hunger of Memory*. New York: Random House.

Rorty, A. (1998). "Rousseau's Education Experiments." In A. Rorty (ed.), *Philosophies of Education* (pp. 238–254). London: Routledge.

Rorty, R. (1998). *Achieving Our Country: Leftist Thought in Twentieth-Century America*. Cambridge, MA: Harvard University Press.

Rorty, R. (1999). *Philosophy and Social Hope*. New York: Penguin.

Rothenberg, D. (2002). *Always the Mountains*. Athens: University of Georgia Press.

Rothenberg, D., & Ulvaeus, M. (eds.) (2001). *The World and the Wild*. Tucson: University of Arizona Press.

Rousseau, J. J. (1953). *The Confessions*. London: Penguin.

Rousseau, J. J. (1979). *Emile, or On Education*. Trans. Allan Bloom. New York: Basic Books.

Ruitenberg, C. (2005). "Deconstructing the Experience of the Local: Towards a Radical Pedagogy of Place." In K. Howe (ed.), *Philosophy of Education* (pp. 212–220). Urbana, IL: Philosophy of Education Society.

Sakofs, M. (2001). "Perspectives I Shouldn't Have Done It. Next Time I Won't." *Journal of Experiential Education*, *24*(1), 5–6.

Savage, G. (2010). "Problematizing 'Public Pedagogy' in Educational Research." In J. Sandlin, B. Schultz, & J. Burdick (eds.), *Handbook of Public Pedagogy: Education and Learning Beyond Schooling* (p. 103). New York: Routledge.

Schubert, W. H., Schubert, A. L. L., Thomas, T. P., & Carroll, W. (2002). *Curriculum Books: The First Hundred Years*. New York: Peter Lang.

Scott, J. (1991). "The Evidence of Experience." *Critical Inquiry*, *1*(7), 773–797.

Seaman, J. (2008). "Experience, Reflect, Critique: The End of the 'Learning Cycles' Era." *Experiential Education, 31*(1), 3–18.

Seaman, J., & Gass, M. (2004). "Service-Learning and Outdoor Education: Promising Reform Movements or Future Relics?" *Journal of Experiential Education, 27*(1), 20.

Shellenberger, M., & Nordhaus, T. (2005). "The Death of Environmentalism: Global Warming Politics in a Post-Environmental World." *Grist Magazine* http://www.grist.org/article/doe-reprint.

Shor, I. (1992). *Empowering Education: Critical Teaching for Social Change.* Chicago: University of Chicago Press.

Shor, I., & Freire, P. (1987). *A Pedagogy for Liberation: Dialogues on Transforming Education.* South Hadley, MA: Bergin & Garvey.

Sizer, T. R. (1997). *Horace's School.* Boston: Houghton Mifflin.

Smith, L. T. (2005). "On Tricky Ground: Researching the Native in the Age of Uncertainty." In N. Denzin & Y. Lincoln (eds.), *The Sage Handbook of Qualitative Research* (pp. 85–107). London: Sage.

Snyder, G. (1990). *The Practice of the Wild.* San Francisco: North Point Press.

Sobel, D. (2005). *Place-based Education: Connecting Classrooms & Communities.* Great Barrington, MA: Orion Society.

Soulé, M. E., Lease, G., & Gussow, A. (1995). *Reinventing Nature?: Responses to Postmodern Deconstruction.* Washington, DC: Island Press.

Stanton, T., Giles, D., & Cruz, N. (1999). *Service-Learning.* San Francisco: Jossey-Bass Publishers.

Thoreau, H. D. (2004). *The Maine Woods (Writings of Henry D. Thoreau).* Princeton: Princeton University Press.

Trinh T. Minh-ha (1986). "Introduction." *Discourse: Journal for Theoretical Studies in Media and Culture, 8* (Fall/Winter), 7–10.

Turner, J. (1996). *The Abstract Wild.* Tucson: University of Arizona Press.

Warren, K., Mitten, D., & Loeffler, T. A. (eds.). (1995). *The Theory and Practice of Experiential Education.* Boulder: Association for Experiential Education.

Warren, K., Mitten, D., & Loeffler, T. A. (eds.). (2008). *The Theory and Practice of Experiential Education.* Boulder: Association for Experiential Education.

Weber, M. (1930). *The Protestant Ethic and the Spirit of Capitalism,* translated by Talcott Parsons. London: Unwin Hyman.

Weber, M. (1947). *The Theory of Economic and Social Organization,* translated by A.M. Henderson and Talcott Parsons. New York: Oxford University Press.

West, C. (1989). *The American Evasion of Philosophy: A Genealogy of Pragmatism.* Madison, WI: University of Wisconsin Press.

West, C. (2000). Remarks to the Coalition of Essential Schools Fall Forum. Retrieved April 8, 2009, from http://www.essentialschools.org/pub/ces_docs/fforum/2000/speeches/west_00.

White, R. (1995). "'Are You an Environmentalist or Do You Work for a Living?': Work and Nature." *Uncommon Ground: Toward Reinventing Nature,* 171–185.

White, S. (2004). "The Very Idea of a Critical Social Science: A Pragmatist Turn." In F. Rush (ed.), *The Cambridge Companion to Critical Theory* (pp. 310–335). New York: Cambridge University Press.

Whitman, Walt (1900). *Leaves of Grass.* Philadelphia: David McKay.

Wolcott, H. (1997). "The Teacher as an Enemy." In G. Spindler (ed.), *Education and Cultural Process: Anthropological Approaches* (pp. 136–156). Long Grove, IL: Waveland Press.

INDEX

Note: Page numbers followed by 'n' refer to notes.

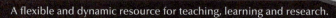